CROCHET Squared

MARSHA A. POLK

25 easy crochet projects made from simple squares

NORTH LIGHT BOOKS
CINCINNATI, OHIO
www.artistsnetwork.com

10   09   08   07   06   5   4   3   2   1

Distributed in Canada by Fraser Direct
100 Armstrong Avenue
Georgetown, ON, Canada L7G 5S4
Tel: (905) 877–4411

Distributed in the U.K. and Europe by David & Charles
Brunel House, Newton Abbot, Devon, TQ12 4PU, England
Tel: (+44) 1626 323200, Fax: (+44) 1626 323319
Email: postmaster@davidandcharles.co.uk

Distributed in Australia by Capricorn Link
P.O. Box 704, S. Windsor, NSW 2756 Australia
Tel: (02) 4577-3555

Library of Congress Cataloging-in-Publication Data
Polk, Marsha.
  Crochet squared : 25 easy projects made from simple squares / Marsha Polk.
       p. cm.
  Includes index.
  ISBN-13: 978-1-58180-833-9 (alk. paper)
  ISBN-10: 1-58180-833-X (alk. paper)
  1. Crocheting--Patterns. I. Title.
  TT825.P63 2006
  746.43'4--dc22

                                            2006002634

![fw F+W PUBLICATIONS, INC.]

Editor: Jessica Gordon
Art Director: Marissa Bowers
Layout Artist: Jessica Schultz
Production Coordinator: Greg Nock
Photographers: Al Parrish and Christine Polomsky
Photo Stylist: Leslie Brinkley

DEDICATION

This book is dedicated to my family and friends. You've listened to me talk about yarn and crochet for a lifetime. You'll be happy to know that now you can read about it, too.

MEET MARSHA

Marsha A. Polk is proprietress of MAP Fiber Creations. A self-taught fiber artist, Marsha has been knitting, crocheting, weaving and making jewelry for over 25 years. Marsha works with the finest materials from around the world and combines unique elements of color, texture, fiber and design to create unique garments. The finished pieces are conversation-stopping works of wearable art that take on the mood and persona of their wearer.

Marsha sits on the professional critique panel for knitwear design at the University of Cincinnati College of Design, Art and Architecture and teaches designer crochet at yarn and specialty shops across the country. Marsha's work can be found in galleries, trunk shows, specialty boutiques and online (www.goodhandarts.com). You can also find Marsha's work at the Cincinnati Art Museum. Marsha is a member of the creative design team at Fibergé, a fiber specialty shop in Terrace Park, Ohio; a member of the professional branch of the Crochet Guild of America; and a member of the American Craft Council. In addition, Marsha has her own line of creative knit and crochet patterns. She designs and creates her original pieces of wearable art in her Amberley Village, Ohio studio.

ACKNOWLEDGMENTS

Thanks to the source of all good gifts for giving me the ability to put it all together.
Thanks to Marty, Martin and Michael. You spent hours at yarn shops without complaining—well, you spent hours, anyway. You've provided me with the support and encouragement to pursue this project.

Thanks to Mom for all the obvious reasons.

Thanks to Kim for feverishly crocheting and testing my pattern designs.

Thanks to Aunt Aileen and Vallarie for wearing my pieces with style and flair.

Thanks to Liz, who kept me going when I didn't think I was "worthy."

Thanks to Cindy for inspiration support.

Thanks to Lori, Sandy and Marcie for "deep" conversations and artistic support.

Thanks to Rudy, Ray, Shirley, Jewel, Nicole, and Miyohnna for encouragement and endless laughs.

Thanks to Debbie and Alicia; you believed in me when I didn't believe in myself.

Thanks to Vickie for unconditional friendship.

Thanks to Enesha and Miriam. Your modeling skills add life to my work.

Special thanks to Alysia. You were there to help and support me from the beginning. I will always be grateful to my "adopted daughter."

Thanks to the staff at F+W. You believed in me and in this project—I couldn't have done it without you.

Contents

GET HIP TO SQUARES — 7

HOOK, LINE AND SINKER: — 8
Choosing the Right Crochet Hook, Yarn and Project

CROCHET 101 — 14

BODY WRAPS — 32

Kimmy-Kimmy KoKo Pop Silk Scarf 34
Berries and Champagne Shawl 37
Penny-for-Your-Thoughts Copper Beaded Body Drape 38
Red Hot Body Drape 41
Kathleen's Peacock Ponshawl 42
The Grass Is Greener Ponshawl 46
Pride and Soy Ponshawl 47
Claudia's Hand Shrawl 48
Ocean Mist Shrawl 52
Orange You Glad Shrawl 53
Painter's Palette Poncho 54
Miter Square Shrawl 58

ACCESSORIES — 62

Bouncing Baby Boy Cardigan + Cap 64
Vickie's Bad Hair Day Hat 68
Miriam's Savvy Chenille Hat 71
"That's My Baby" Booties 72
Green Peas and Grape Juice
    Baby Sweater and Booties 75
Vallarie's Royal Slippers 76
Pastel Paradise Slippers 79
Jessica-Loves-Chocolate Purse 80
Yoruba Handbag 83
Let's-Go-Shopping Tote 84

SHELLS, CARDIGANS + JACKETS — 88

Deep Blue Sea Beaded Shell 90
Sparkling Grape Juice Shell 94
Mildred's Stained Glass Window
    Short-Sleeved Cardigan 98
Regina's Gold Cropped Jacket 102
Ice Cream with Rainbow Sprinkles Vest 105
Lizzy's Night Out Jacket 106
Nutmeg and Cinnamon Jacket 111
Strawberries and Cream in Paris
    Long-Sleeved Jacket 112

USEFUL INFORMATION — 120

Abbreviations 120
Crochet Hook Conversions 121
Substituting Yarns 122
Fiber Art: A Poem 123
Crocheting on the Web 125

RESOURCES — 124   INDEX — 126

Get Hip to Squares

■ ■ ■ I HAVE BEEN CROCHETING for over twenty-five years, and I've watched the art of crochet evolve from a regimented craft into an avant-garde expression of design and creativity. I have experienced varying reactions to crochet during my decades of design, and I am happy to see it emerge as the "must-do" craft of the 21st century.

Of course, not everyone knows how hip crochet is. Even today, mention of crochet inevitably brings visions of granny squares and afghans. While I have nothing against the granny square, crochet has so much more to offer. Crochet is now recognized as one of the most progressive forms of fiber art. Throughout the pages of this book, I will bring you specially designed, unique pieces that add crochet flair to the crochet square. If you were bitten by the "scarf bug" and are now ready to create fashion-forward garments and accessories, this book is for you. If you can make a scarf, you can complete any of the projects in this book. All of the body wraps, accessories, shells and jackets are simple to construct and feature many of the hot new yarns and fibers found in your local yarn shop.

In *Crochet Squared*, we will use only the chain and single crochet stitch. And, to keep things as simple as possible, all the projects are constructed from a square (not your granny's) or a rectangle. Then, to really get you hooked, in most instances you will use a large crochet hook. In no time at all, you will create beautiful crochet masterpieces. For those of you who haven't yet (notice I said *yet*) mastered the art of crochet, a square is a square no matter what stitch you use. As Valentina Devine, fiber artist extraordinaire and master of creative crochet, said after viewing one of my crochet masterpieces, "You are creating interesting pieces of fabric—the stitch doesn't care if it is knit or crochet." While this book is designed for the crocheter, the "stitch doesn't know," so knitters too can apply my techniques to garter stitch or other simple knit patterns.

Marsha's Corner

Throughout the book, look for Marsha's Corner, where I'll pass on to you the special techniques, topics for discussion or thoughts I have gleaned during my twenty-five-plus years of crocheting.

Hook, Line and Sinker

Before you chain your first stitch, you need to know a few bits of essential information. I think of these basic elements as the hook, line and sinker. The hook is the beginning of the crochet process. Then you'll need a line (yarn or fiber) to form stitches and ultimately create fabric. The sinker is the culmination of factors that ultimately influences how we select projects and fibers and what we do with the finished piece.

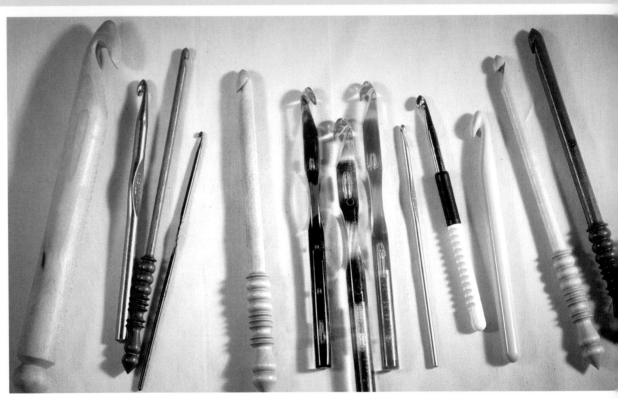

Hooks of all shapes, sizes and materials, from left to right: *large wooden hook, medium-sized metal hook, small wooden hook with decorative handle, extra small metal crochet hook for attaching beads and paillettes, medium-sized wooden hook with decorative handle, plastic hooks in various sizes, small metal hook, metal hook with rubber grip, large plastic hook, wooden hooks.*

Hook

Because crochet hooks come in so many sizes, colors, shapes and materials, choosing one is a matter of personal preference. Try a few different kinds of hooks and select what's right for you. But how will you know when you've found your perfect match? In my experience, hooks made of metal, glass or plastic work best for experienced crocheters who stitch quickly. Wooden hooks tend to create a little more friction and may be more suitable for a beginner. Hook sizes are given in three different ways: letter size, number size and millimeter size. In my many years of crocheting, I've found that there are often discrepancies between sizes from hook to hook. I've chosen to list only the millimeter size, because it is the most accurate. Please see the chart in the Useful Information section, page 121, for more information on hook sizing.

HOLDING YOUR HOOK

At times, the way you hold your hook can influence the type of hook you select. Traditionalists say there are two ways to hold your hook: Like a knife when cutting food (my method of choice...I wonder why?) or like a pencil when writing. However, I have noticed a new generation of crocheters who have their own unique way of holding a crochet hook. The stitch doesn't care how you hold your hook. What matters is that you are able to make a stitch, no matter how you hold the hook. Some hooks have carved designs or grooves at the base. Those designs may not be comfortable for the crocheter who holds her hook like a knife because the designs in the hook press on the hand and can interfere with your rhythm.

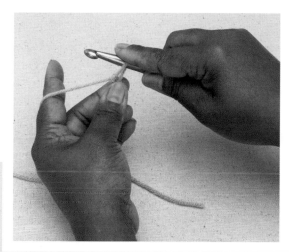

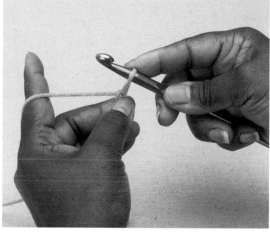

HOLDING YOUR HOOK LIKE A KNIFE

When holding the hook like a knife, your hand should make a loose fist on top of the hook, with the pointer finger resting lightly on top of the loop on the hook to guide the stitches.

HOLDING YOUR HOOK LIKE A PENCIL

When holding the hook like a pencil, your thumb and index finger should grasp the hook toward the top (as if to write with the hook). The remaining fingers should be in a loose fist at the bottom of the hook.

Marsha's Corner

If you hold your hook like a knife, or if you have large hands, look for longer hooks. A longer shaft allows more room to grasp your hook as you make your stitches.

Line

When I'm admiring a wondrous work of art, one question always comes to mind: "How did the artist put those materials together to come up with such a beautiful masterpiece?" My designs always start with inspiration. By definition, inspiration can be a supposed force or influence on artists. Inspiration can also mean stimulating creative activity or exalted thoughts. It can be a person or principle, either abstract or concrete. At the most basic level, inspiration can be defined as the drawing in of breath. That last, simple definition correlates with the concept that inspiration comes from living and breathing. Whatever crosses your path can be an inspiration if you take the time to experience it.

So what does all this have to do with selecting yarn? Everything! The 21st century has fueled a revolution in fiber arts—we are living in the aftermath of a fiber explosion. Each visit to the local yarn shop is like a fine feast. With so many choices, where do you begin? Hanks, balls, skeins. Ribbons, eyelash, fur. Slub, boucle, smooth. Wool, silk, cashmere. These are but a few of the tasty morsels now available in the yarn world. In this section, you'll learn the difference between one kind of yarn and another and you'll also learn how to choose the best yarn for your project.

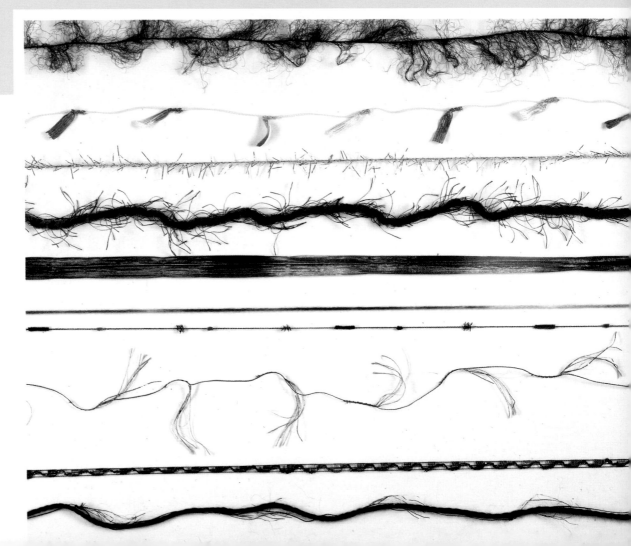

Yarns of all kinds, from top to bottom: *fur, flag lash, short eyelash, novelty, ribbon, smooth worsted weight, strander, thread eyelash, ladder, smooth and eyelash combination.*

CHOOSING YARN

When selecting yarn, I suggest you begin with inspiration in its simplest form. You may have a pattern with a suggested yarn and that's all the inspiration you need. In that case, all the legwork has been done for you, and you merely need to find the matching yarn for the pattern in hand. At times, inspiration may come from simple objects, surroundings, or life itself. Are you inspired by a button, sculpture, painting, article of clothing, piece of jewelry, musical beat, color combination, textures, facial expressions, a baby's hair...Get the idea? Your fiber selection can also be inspired by a few simple questions: What season is it? What color(s) appeal to me? How many shades of green (or brown if your gardening skills are like mine) do I see in the grass? When I look at a magazine, what objects jump out at me? What textures are visually appealing to me? Once you're in the yarn shop, look around and find the yarns and fibers that match the answers to the above questions.

Marsha's Corner

Just like some foods are easier on the digestion, some yarns are easier to crochet. In general, smooth, non-textured yarns are the easiest to crochet. However, larger hooks and certain combinations of smooth and textured fiber make crocheting with novelty yarns fun and fast.

HOLDING YOUR YARN

You must get a good grip on your yarn in order to establish a steady crochet rhythm, a term that refers to the flow or pace of making crochet stitches. The yarn should flow smoothly, allowing for an even tension. The following photos demonstrate how I hold yarn when crocheting. You can use my method or try any other way you like. The key is for the yarn to move easily and freely to form uniform crochet stitches.

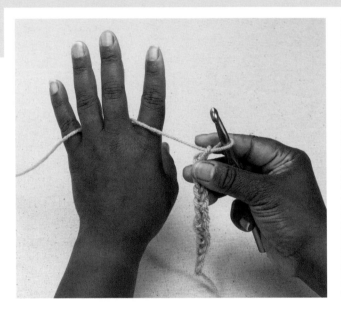

WEAVE YARN OVER AND UNDER FINGERS

Holding the hook in your right hand, weave the yarn on top of baby finger, under your hand and on top of your index finger.

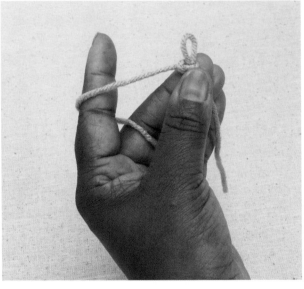

HOLD WORK

As you begin to work your stitches, fold your two middle fingers around the yarn and sandwich the working fabric between your thumb and middle fingers. The index finger remains free to keep a consistent tautness in the yarn as you work.

Marsha's Corner

I suggest starting with the Kimmy-Kimmy KoKo Pop silk scarf or the Bouncing Baby Boy Cap. Build your crochet confidence by beginning with a simple project you'll be able to complete quickly. You'll soon be ready to tackle larger and more difficult projects.

Sinker

In the Hook and Line sections, you've learned the basic information you need to select a hook and yarn for your first project. Before you turn the page and enroll in Crochet 101, there are a few bits of information you'll find useful as you make the projects in this book.

SELECTING A PROJECT

Crochet Squared simplifies the sometimes "weighty" process of selecting yarn and projects. I've done the legwork for you in choosing yarn, and I've even arranged the sections to simplify project selection. The book starts with basic scarf-like projects designed to provide immediate gratification, and advances by section to more challenging creations. In addition, the projects within each section progress from the easiest to more challenging. However, every project is a basic square or rectangle, so a beginner can complete any selection.

READING A PATTERN

What do all those mysterious letters mean? It's really quite simple, once you have a "translation" like the one here. When you understand crochet language, reading a pattern is easy. For example, a pattern might read:

FOUNDATION CHAIN: Ch 53. *(Make a chain of 53.)*

Row 1: Work 1 sc in second ch from hook and in each rem ch (52 sts). Ch 1 and turn work.
(Insert your hook into the second chain and single crochet 52 stitches, make one chain and turn work.)

Row 2: Work 1 sc in each of the next 25 sts, sk 2, work 1 sc in each of the rem 25 sts, ch 1 and turn work.
(Single crochet 25 stitches, skip 2 stitches, single crochet 25 stitches, make one chain stitch and turn work.)

Crochet 101

Making a Slip Knot

Making a slip knot is always the first step in the crochet process.
All crochet stitches start with this humble loop.

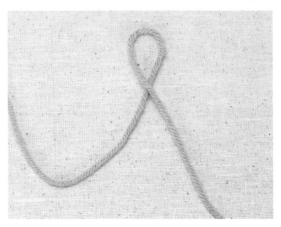

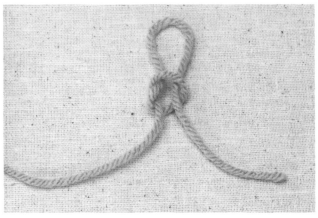

1. MAKE LOOP WITH YARN

To begin a slip knot, cross the end of the yarn over
itself to create a loop. Leave at least a 3" (8cm) tail.

2. PULL YARN THROUGH LOOP

Double up the yarn attached to the ball just below the
loop from step one. Pull that loop through the loop you
created in step one. Pull on the tails to adjust the size
of the loop.

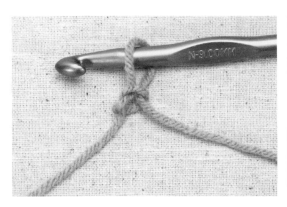

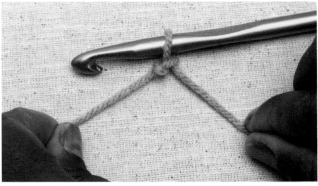

3. SLIDE HOOK THROUGH SLIP KNOT

Get ready to make your first chain stitch by sliding
the hook through the loose slip knot.

4. TIGHTEN SLIP KNOT

Tighten the slip knot around the hook by pulling on both
strands of yarn. The slip knot should be snug, but it
should still have enough room to slide back and forth on
the hook easily.

Making a Chain

The chain is the foundation of any crocheted fabric. Be careful not to create a chain that's too tight. It is difficult to get the hook through a tight chain, and it can hinder your ability to form stitches.

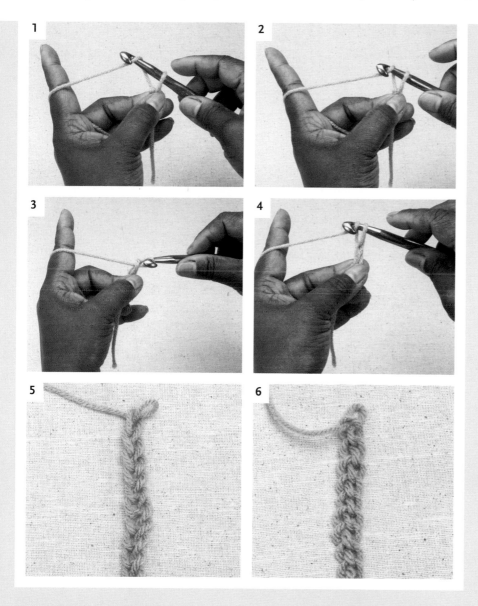

1. WRAP YARN

Once you have the tightened slip knot on your hook, wrap the end of yarn that's attached to the ball or skein around the hook. This action is also called a yarn over (yo). Keep your work steady by holding the yarn tail between your thumb and middle finger.

2. GRAB YARN AND BEGIN TO PULL THROUGH

Grab the wrapped yarn with the hook and begin to pull the yarn back toward the slip knot.

3. CREATE FIRST CHAIN STITCH

Pull the wrapped yarn through the slip knot to create the first chain stitch.

4. CONTINUE TO MAKE CHAIN

Continue to make chain stitches by wrapping the yarn around the hook from back to front and pulling it through the existing loop with the tip of the hook. There should always be only one loop on your hook when you have finished making a chain or stitch.

5. FRONT OF CHAIN

I always put my hook through the front of the chain. The front of the chain looks like a line of v's or like a braid.

6. BACK OF CHAIN

The back of a crochet chain is bumpy and looks like a row of ants or camel humps.

Marsha's Corner

If you have difficulty getting the hook into the chain, then you are probably a "tight crocheter." To avoid a foundation chain that's too tight, try using a hook that is one or two sizes larger than the instructions call for to make the starting chain. Then switch to the crochet hook the pattern calls for as you begin the first row.

Single Crochet Stitch

All the projects in *Crochet Squared* use the single crochet stitch, which is, fittingly, a square itself. After the chain stitch, single crochet is usually the first stitch beginners learn. Once you've mastered this stitch, you can create almost any crochet masterpiece. Don't forget to chain one at the end of each row of single crochet before starting the next row.

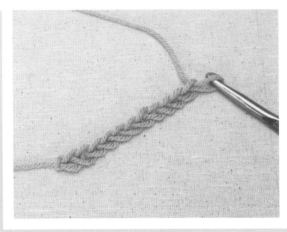

1. MAKE CHAIN

Make a chain to form the base of the crocheted object (see pages 14–15). The chain is one more than the number of stitches you will end up with. There will always be at least one loop on your hook at any point in the crocheting process.

2. LOCATE SECOND CHAIN FROM HOOK

Locate the second chain from the hook by counting two of the v's directly after the loop on the hook, as indicated by the red hook.

3. INSERT HOOK INTO SECOND CHAIN FROM HOOK

Insert the hook into the second chain from the hook, sliding the hook through the top leg of the v from front to back.

4. GRAB YARN WITH HOOK AND PULL THROUGH

When you insert the hook into the chain, the yarn will lay naturally across the hook. Grab the yarn and pull it through the stitch. As you grab the yarn with the hook, hold the chain steady by grasping the chain between your thumb and index finger.

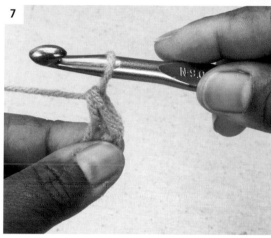

5. COUNT TWO LOOPS ON HOOK

Make sure you have two loops on your hook, as shown.

6. WRAP YARN AROUND HOOK

Wrap the yarn around the hook (yo). There are two loops and one yarn wrap on the hook.

7. PULL YARN THROUGH BOTH LOOPS

Pull the wrapped yarn through both of the loops on the hook. There will be one loop on your hook when you have completed a single crochet stitch.

8. FINISH FIRST ROW OF SINGLE CROCHET

When you finish the first single crochet stitch, insert the hook into the next chain from front to back. Repeat steps four through seven until you finish the row, taking care not to twist the chain.

9. CHECK WORK

When you finish the first row, check your work by making sure that the yarn tail is at the left bottom of your work.

Marsha's Corner

When I make a yarn over, I always wrap my yarn from back to front around the hook. Some crocheters prefer to wrap the yarn from front to back. Either way produces a fine single crochet stitch. Choose the manner of wrapping that feels best to you.

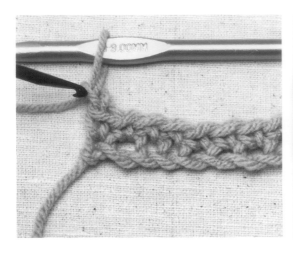

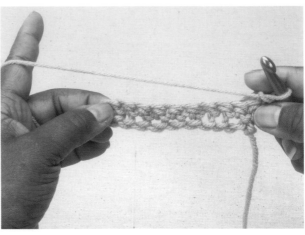

10. MAKE CHAIN STITCH

Before turning your work, make a single chain by wrapping the yarn around the hook and pulling it through the existing loop, as shown on page 15. The chain above is indicated by the red hook. In a pattern, this is written as "ch 1."

11. TURN WORK

To begin the next row, turn your work so the yarn tail is at the right bottom of your work. In a pattern, this is written as "turn work" or simply "turn."

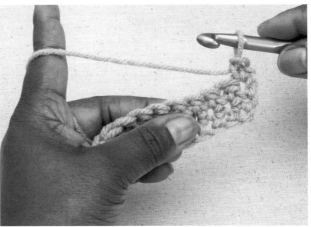

12. BEGIN SECOND ROW

For the second row of single crochet, and for each subsequent row, you'll slide the hook from front to back through both legs of each stitch that make up the v in the previous row. You may hold your work with thumb and index finger to keep it steady.

13. CONTINUE TO MAKE SINGLE CROCHET STITCHES

Continue to make single crochet stitches in the same way you made them in the first row. Remember to ch 1 at the end of each row before turning your work.

Holding Two Yarns Together

Many of the projects in *Crochet Squared* require you to crochet with two different yarns held together and worked as one fiber. Crocheting with two strands can increase the gauge, and also enables you to work more easily with eyelash and specialty yarns. It can also add textural interest to the crocheted fabric.

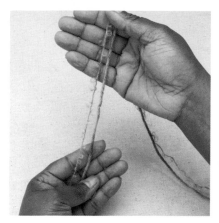

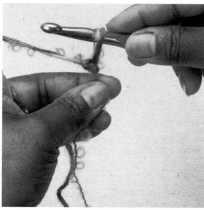

1. HOLD YARNS SIDE BY SIDE

Choose the yarns you'd like to use together and match them up.

2. MAKE SLIP KNOT WITH YARNS TOGETHER

Make a slip knot with both yarns together and tighten the knot around the hook.

3. MAKE CHAIN STITCH

Make a chain holding the two yarns together.

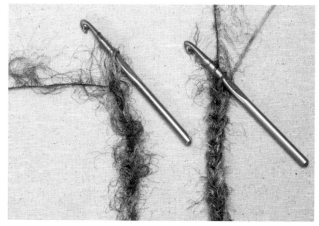

4. BEGIN SINGLE CROCHET

Follow the same steps as when working with a single strand to begin a single crochet fabric. As you can see in the image above, as you stitch, the individual strands become less and less visible.

WORKING WITH EYELASH YARN

When working with eyelash yarn, you can crochet it by itself or work it together with another yarn to create a different look. As you can see from this image, eyelash yarn by itself (left) has very little stitch definition. When worked together with a smoother yarn (right), the stitches are much more visible, making crocheting a little easier.

Crocheting with Paillettes and Beads

Another way to add color or textural interest is to crochet with paillettes (large sequins) or beads.
Both can be used throughout a project for an all-over beaded effect, or they can be attached to the
fabric randomly for just a bit of sparkle. Both can also be used to embellish the hem of a jacket or the
ends of a scarf. While there are several techniques for crocheting with beads and paillettes, I use one
simple method, as outlined here. You will crochet with the hook required by the pattern, and switch
to a much smaller hook to add the bead or paillette.

CROCHETING WITH PAILLETTES

1. INSERT SMALL HOOK INTO LOOP

Decide where you want to place the paillettes and create
crocheted fabric up to that point. At the spot where you
want to add a paillette, slide the larger hook out of the
loop and set it aside. Insert a smaller hook (one that will
fit through the hole in the paillette) into the loop.

2. SLIDE PAILLETTE ONTO HOOK

Slide a paillette onto the small crochet hook.
There is one loop and one paillette on the hook.

3. SLIDE HOOK THROUGH STITCH

Slide the small hook through the next stitch, just as you
would when making a regular single crochet stitch.

4. PULL LOOP THROUGH PAILLETTE

Pull the loop on your hook through the paillette,
leaving two loops on the crochet hook.

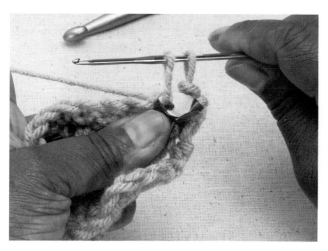

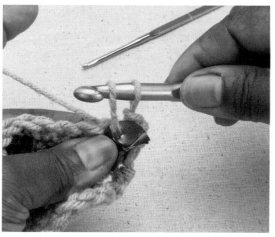

5. COUNT TWO LOOPS ON HOOK

There are now two loops on the crochet hook, and the paillete is part of the crocheted fabric.

6. SWITCH TO LARGER HOOK

Remove the small hook from the loops and switch to the larger hook.

7. FINISH SINGLE CROCHET

Finish the single crochet stitch by wrapping the yarn once more and pulling it through both loops, leaving one loop on the hook.

8. FINISH ROW

Continue to attach paillettes, spacing them as desired.

Marsha's Corner

Plan in advance where beads or paillettes will be placed. Then there are no surprises or accents on eye-catching parts of the body.

CROCHETING WITH BEADS

To crochet with beads, follow the same basic steps as for crocheting with paillettes. Just remember to make sure that your small hook can fit completely through the bead hole.

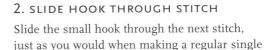

1. SLIDE BEAD ONTO HOOK

Decide where you want to place the beads and create crocheted fabric up to that point. At the spot where you want to add a bead, slide the larger hook out of the loop and set it aside. Insert a smaller hook (one that will fit through the hole in the bead) into the loop. Slide a bead onto the crochet hook.

2. SLIDE HOOK THROUGH STITCH

Slide the small hook through the next stitch, just as you would when making a regular single crochet stitch.

3. WRAP YARN AROUND HOOK AND PULL LOOP THROUGH

Wrap the yarn around the hook from back to front. Grab the yarn with the hook and pull it through the first loop. You will now have one loop, a bead, and another loop on your hook.

4. PULL YARN THROUGH BEAD

Wrap the yarn around the hook again. Grab the yarn with the hook and pull it through the first loop and the bead.

5. COUNT TWO LOOPS ON HOOK

Switch to the larger hook. Make sure you have two loops on the hook.

6. FINISH SINGLE CROCHET STITCH

Yarn over and pull the wrapped yarn through both of the loops on the hook. There will be one loop on your hook when you finish the stitch.

7. FINISH FIRST ROW OF BEADED SINGLE CROCHET

After adding the first bead, make at least one single crochet stitch before adding another bead. Repeat steps 1 through 7 until you finish the row. After crocheting a row of beads, crochet at least one row without beads, or stagger the bead placement on the next row.

Adding Fringe

Several of the projects in this book incorporate fringe for embellishment. The most basic fringe is made from complementary or contrasting yarn that is attached at the ends of the garment in individual strands. To make a fuller fringe like tassel fringe, simply hold several strands together and attach them all at the same point. For additional embellishment, you may even add beads or paillettes to your fringe.

BASIC FRINGE

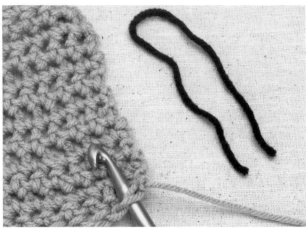

1. CUT FRINGE

Figure out how long you'd like your fringe to be and then cut pieces of yarn to twice that length (the fringe is attached doubled-up). There are also special products for measuring and making fringe.

2. INSERT HOOK

Slide your hook through the first stitch at the edge of your crocheted piece.

3. THREAD FRINGE ONTO HOOK

Fold a piece of fringe yarn in half and slide the doubled-up end onto the hook.

4. GRAB YARN WITH HOOK AND PULL THROUGH

Grab the yarn with the hook and pull the doubled-up end through the stitch.

5. GRAB TAILS WITH HOOK AND PULL THROUGH

Grab the tails of the fringe with your hook and pull them all the way through the loop.

6. TIGHTEN FRINGE INTO PLACE

Tighten the fringe into place by pulling on the tails firmly with your fingers.

7. ATTACH FRINGE

Continue to attach fringe, beginning with the ends and moving to the middle. Attach the next fringe in the middle of two of the other fringes, as indicated by the red hook. Continue attaching fringe in this manner.

8. FINISH ATTACHING FRINGE

Continue to attach fringe until they fill out the crocheted edge.

9. TRIM FRINGE

Use a pair of scissors to trim up the ends of the fringe so they are even.

1. CUT FRINGE AND DOUBLE UP

Cut pieces of fringe as you did for single-strand fringe and double them up in a group of about three strands, or as full as you'd like the tassel to be.

2. ATTACH FIRST TASSEL

Attach the first tassel on one end of the crocheted object by sliding your hook through the first stitch, pulling the looped ends through the stitch and pulling the tails of the fringes through the loop, just as for the single-strand fringe (see pages 24–25). Pull the tassel tight by pulling on the ends with your fingers.

3. CONTINUE ADDING TASSELS

Continue adding fringe on the ends and in the middle, filling in as with the single-strand fringe (pages 24–25).

Individual Beaded Fringe

1. SLIP HOOK THROUGH STITCH

Slip your crochet hook through the stitch where you'd like to attach a beaded dangle.

2. SLIDE LOOP ONTO HOOK

Slip the loop of the beaded tassel onto the crochet hook.

3. PULL LOOP THROUGH STITCH

Use the hook to pull the loop through the stitch.

4. PULL BEADED ENDS THROUGH LOOP

Remove the hook and pull the beaded ends through the loop by hand.

5. FINISH BEADED FRINGE

Tighten the fringe to finish. Add as many beaded fringes as you like.

Changing Colors

Although there are many ways to change yarn colors, all of the patterns in this book change at the end of a row. Since most color-changing methods leave a tell-tale tail, many expert crocheters recommend weaving in the tail or crocheting over it. I am breaking the rules by suggesting that you knot the ends. This is the method I use most, particularly when the garment will be seamed later. This may spark some crochet controversy, but it has worked for me for over 20 years. I haven't had a knot come undone in a finished piece yet.

1. CUT YARN

On the last stitch of the first color, crochet until there are two loops left on your hook. Cut the yarn about 3" (8cm) from the hook.

2. ADD SECOND COLOR

Introduce the second color by holding onto the end with your fingers and wrapping it around the hook. Continue to hold on to the tail of the first color of yarn as well.

3. PULL NEW COLOR THROUGH LOOPS

Grab the new color of yarn with the hook and pull it through the two loops on the hook. One loop of yarn (the new color) should now be on the hook. Continue to hold onto the tails of both colors of yarn.

4. TIE OFF ENDS

Tie the tail of the old color and the tail of the new color of yarn together in a firm knot. Cut off the ends of the yarn close to the knot.

5. CONTINUE CROCHETING IN NEW COLOR

Once the ends are knotted together, continue to single crochet as usual.

Joining Squares with Single Crochet Seam

To join separate crocheted pieces together, I use a simple single crochet seam. I like this method because the seam is hardly visible on the right side of the fabric. Another method involves using a darning needle to stitch seams together. You may also sew your seams on a sewing machine, but this tends to leave some bulk at the joined edges.

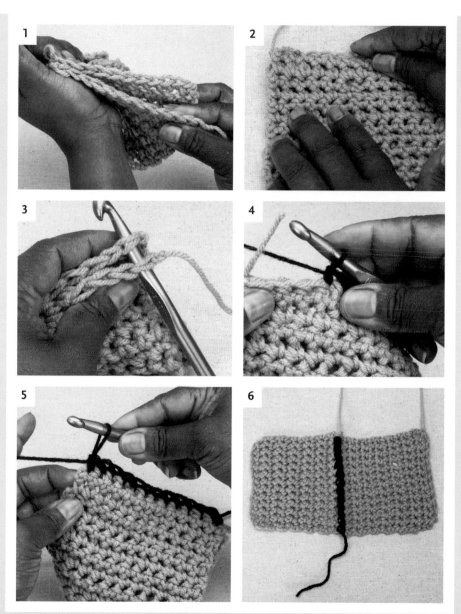

1. LINE UP EDGES

To begin sewing your squares together, line up the edges so the v's match up.

2. PIN EDGES IN PLACE

Once you've matched up the edges, pin them in place with straight pins.

3. BRING HOOK THROUGH FIRST STITCHES

Bring the hook through the first stitches in both crocheted pieces.

4. MAKE FIRST SINGLE CROCHET STITCH

Make a slip knot and slide it onto the hook. Pull the hook through the crocheted pieces. Wrap the yarn around the hook from back to front and make one single crochet stitch.

5. FINISH SEAMING

Continue to bring the hook through both pieces of fabric and single crochet until you reach the end. Cut the yarn and bring the tail through the loop. Pull on the end of the yarn to tighten it.

6. FINISHED SEAM

When you are finished, the two squares will be joined as shown. Of course, on your work the seam will be almost invisible because you will use yarn that is the same color as the crocheted fabric to create the seam. I've used a contrasting color yarn to make it easy for you to see the seam.

Weaving in Ends

I generally use a crochet hook to weave in yarn tails. The hook is handy and works well for grabbing yarn tails and pulling them through the crocheted fabric. A tapestry needle works just as well, but you'll need to remember to leave a long enough tail to thread through the needle and weave.

1. BRING HOOK THROUGH CROCHETED FABRIC

Bring the crochet hook through the crocheted fabric very close to the end of yarn that you will be weaving in.

2. PULL YARN THROUGH

Hook the yarn tail and begin to pull it through the crocheted fabric (the yarn will form a loop on your hook).

3. TIGHTEN YARN

Remove the hook from the loop and pull the yarn tail through it. Tighten the knot by pulling on the tail.

4. CONTINUE WEAVING IN END

Continue to weave in the tail, repeating steps 1 through 3 until you run out of yarn.

5. FINISHED FABRIC

Once the ends of the yarn are woven in, the crocheted fabric will look smooth and finished.

Miter Square

The miter square is a simple way to create complex designs. It starts with a simple shape (the square) and uses it as a building block for creative design. Miter squares can be combined in a number of ways to form intricate pathways of color and texture. On this page, you'll find the basic steps for creating a miter square, as well as row-by-row instructions. See page 58 for a pattern that uses miter squares.

1. BEGIN TO TURN SQUARE

To begin a miter square, chain 25. Starting in the second chain from the hook, work 1 single crochet in each of the next 11 chains. Skip the next two chains, as indicated by the red crochet hook. Work 1 single crochet in each remaining chain (11 stitches).

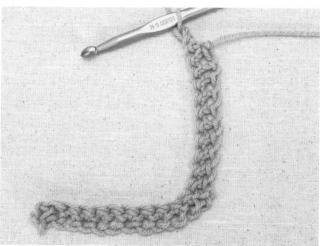

2. TURN SQUARE

When you complete the first row of single crochet, chain once and turn the square, as shown.

3. FINISHED MITER SQUARE

Follow the row-by-row instructions at right to finish the miter square. You may change colors at any point in the process to high-light the construction of the square.

Miter Square Pattern

Follow this simple pattern to crochet a miter square

FOUNDATION CHAIN: Ch 25.

Row 1: Starting in second ch from hook, work 1 sc in each of the next 11 ch, sk 2 ch, and work 1 sc in rem 11 ch. Ch 1 and turn.

Row 2: Work 1 sc in each of the next 10 sts, sk 2, work 1 sc in rem 10 sts. Ch 1 and turn.

Row 3: Work 1 sc in each of the next 9 sts, sk 2, work 1 sc in rem 9 sts. Ch 1 and turn.

Rows 4–10: Decrease the number of sc sts on either side of the 2 skipped sts by 1 each time you finish a row. For example, row 4 will be sc 8, sk 2, sc 8. Keep decreasing each row as established. Always ch 1 at the end of each row before turning work.

FINAL ROW: For your final row, work 1 sc, sk 2 sts, work 1 sc. Ch 1, cut yarn and pull tail through to secure.

BODY WRAPS

■ ■ ■ BODY WRAPS AND BODY DRAPES are my signature designs. They are versatile garments that can be worn in many different ways—as scarves, neck-wraps, sashes, belts, or even as skirts or vests. How you wear your body wrap is limited only by your imagination! In each piece in this section, I've combined color, texture and fiber to create a specially designed, one-of-a-kind piece of wearable art. Every design in this chapter is made up of one or more squares or rectangles. We will start with the basic scarf, made from one long, slender rectangle. Simply enlarge the scarf design to create a body wrap. From there, progress to the *ponshawl*, a cross between a poncho and a shawl, which incorporates strategically placed buttons to provide many options for wear. Finally, we will create a *shrawl*, which combines the style of a shrug with the ease and warmth of a shawl.

Kimmy-Kimmy KoKo Pop
silk scarf

■ ■ ■ I AM THE OLDEST OF THREE CHILDREN. I have a younger brother, and my sister, Kim, is the "baby." Like most older siblings, my brother and I took much delight in finding ways to upset our little sister Kim to the point of tears. Kim learned early how to ignore our various taunts, teases and tickles. When all else failed, my brother and I would resort to singing a popular song, inserting "Kimmy-Kimmy KoKo Pop" in place of the song's lyrics. No matter how hard she tried, Kim could not ignore us as we sang louder and louder. Our little song annoys Kim to this day, and singing it to her still makes me laugh. My sister is very special to me, and I designed this scarf from an equally special hand-dyed silk ribbon.

Yarn

one spool (40 yds) each of 7/16" (1cm) Hannah Silk Ribbon:

Forest Shadows (A)

Sea Cave (B)

Wild Berry (C)

Pink Rosebud (D)

Garnet (E)

Hook

20mm (S or T) crochet hook

Instructions

FOUNDATION CHAIN: Using color A, chain 21.

BLOCK 1: Starting in second ch from hook, work 1 sc in each rem ch (20 sts). Ch 1 and turn work. Cont to work 1 sc in each st (20 sts total) until last complete row can be made with color A.

BLOCK 2: Cut yarn A at end of row and tie on new spool (color B) with a visible knot (the knot is part of the overall embellishment of the scarf and should be placed on the "right" side of the scarf). Work 1 sc in each st (20 sts total). Ch 1 and turn work. Cont to work in sc until last complete row can be made with color B.

BLOCKS 3, 4 AND 5: Cont in sc, changing to colors C, D and E as before, always making 1 sc in each st for a total of 20 sts for each row.

End work by pulling tail of silk through last st, leaving about a 3" (8cm) tail.

Finishing

Cut leftover silk ribbon in the colors of your choice into 15 strips 4" to 5" (10cm to 13cm) long. Knot these strips randomly onto the finished scarf along the edges and in the middle of the scarf. Notice the versatility of this scarf and how it can be worn in many different ways.

BLOCK 1	BLOCK 2	BLOCK 3	BLOCK 4	BLOCK 5
YARN A	YARN B	YARN C	YARN D	YARN E

Berries and Champagne Shawl

At times it's a challenge to find the right wrap for an evening out, and the Berries and Champagne Shawl is the perfect solution. Like Kimmy-Kimmy KoKo Pop, this shawl is a basic scarf—it's simply longer and wider. This variation is crocheted lengthwise using Cherry Tree Hill Fun Fur in Champage and Burgundy stranded with Eros Glitz in Wine Tones (color 960). Using a 15mm hook and two yarns stranded together, crochet a chain that totals the length you want for your shawl. Working in single crochet, make this shawl as wide as you like, or simply work until you run out of yarn. To finish the shawl, first weave in the ends (see Crochet 101, page 30). Finally, add some finishing touches to dress the shawl up. Use a ribbon fringe (such as Eros Extreme Ribbon in Fire [color 3257]) on the short ends (see Crochet 101, pages 24–25), and add paillette trim across one of the long sides (see Crochet 101, pages 20–21). The length of this scarf variation allows you many options for wrapping yourself in luxury.

Penny-for-Your-Thoughts
copper beaded body drape

■ ■ ■ Pennies! in a jar, on the street, they're everywhere. Many don't consider the penny very valuable. Isn't it something that a coin with such richness of color is the "poorest" in value? When I see pennies, I reminisce about the "good old days," back when you could get two pieces of candy for a penny—one for yourself and another to share with a friend. For me, a penny represents priceless memories of children filled with excitement because they just received a penny. A penny represents the many decisions made at the candy counter (each pack of Kits had five pieces, so two packs was enough to share with most of the kids in the neighborhood). Those days are gone, but not forgotten. What better way to capture those memories than in this beautiful beaded drape? Listen as the beads move and make a sound like pennies shaking in a jar. Make one body drape for yourself and one for a friend.

Yarn

4 balls (140 yards each) ¼" (6mm) Filatura Di Crosa Karen ribbon yarn in copper (MC)

1 ball (192 yards) Unger Vegas Metallic Lamé Eyelash (A)

1 ball (72 yards) Trendsetter Eyelash in copper (B)

2 balls (72 yards each) Trendsetter Metal Eyelash in copper (C)

1 ball (72 yards) Trendsetter Flora in copper (D)

Hooks and Notions

15mm crochet hook (smaller hook)

20mm crochet hook (larger hook)

beaded fringe

Instructions

FOUNDATION CHAIN: Holding yarns MC and A together, chain 46.

BLOCK 1: Starting in second ch from hook, with MC and A held together, work 1 sc in each rem ch (45 sts). At end of row, ch 1 and turn work. Cont to work in sc until piece measures 12" (31cm) from beg.

BLOCK 2: Cut yarn A at end of row and add in colors B and C. Holding MC, B and C together, work 1 sc in each st (45 sts). Ch 1 and turn work. Cont to work in sc for 8" (20cm). Piece measures 20" (51cm) from beg.

BLOCK 3: At end of row, cut B and C and tie on A. Holding MC and A together, cont to work 1 sc in each st (45 sts) for 18" (46cm). Piece measures 38" (97cm) from beg.

BLOCK 4: At end of row, cut A and join in C and D. Holding C, D and MC together, work 1 sc across all sts (45 sts). Cont in sc for 8" (20cm). Piece measures 46" (117cm) from beg.

BLOCK 5: At end of row, cut C and D and tie on A. Holding MC and A together, cont to work 1 sc in each st (45 sts) for 10" (25cm). Piece measures 56" (142cm) from beg.

BLOCK 6: At end of row, cut A and tie on C and D. Holding MC, C and D together, cont to work 1 sc across all sts (45 sts) for 5" (13cm). Piece measures 61" (155cm) from beg.

BLOCK 7: At end of row, cut C and D and tie on B. Holding MC and B together, cont to work 1 sc across all sts (45 sts) for 6" (15cm). Piece measures 67" (170cm) from beg.

BLOCK 8: At end of row, cut B and tie on A. Holding MC and A together, cont to work 1 sc across all sts (45 sts) for 8" (20cm). Piece measures 75" (191cm) from beg.

End work by cutting yarn and pulling tails of MC and A through last st.

Finishing

Weave in the loose tails of yarn with a crochet hook (see Crochet 101, page 30). Use pre-beaded fringe to embellish the finished 20" (51cm) ends of the body wrap. Simply attach the beaded fringe to the edges at regular intervals using a crochet hook. (See Crochet 101, page 27.)

START HERE →

BLOCK 1
12" (30cm) MC and A held together

BLOCK 2
8" (20cm) MC, B and C held together

BLOCK 3
18" (46cm) MC and A held together

BLOCK 4
8" (20cm) MC, C and D held together

BLOCK 5
10" (25cm) MC and A held together

BLOCK 6
5" (13cm) MC, C and D held together

BLOCK 7
6" (15cm) MC and B held together

BLOCK 8
8" (20cm) MC and A held together

75" (191CM)

20" (51CM)

Red Hot Body Drape

Just as dramatic and simple to make as the Penny-for-Your-Thoughts, the Red Hot Body Drape uses four balls (220 yards ea.) of Karabella gossamer yarn in Fiesta Red (color 5037) and a 15mm crochet hook. A little eyelash spices things up a bit. This wrap demonstrates that a change in fiber drastically changes the look of a garment. Using a 15mm hook, this dramatic drape is a breeze to crochet. When you finish, add a touch of elegance to this scarf variation by embellishing both ends and one long side with Trendsetter Segue ribbon yarn in black (color 55), or any shiny wide black ribbon. You'll be red hot and ready to party.

Kathleen's Peacock Ponshawl

■■■ THE PEACOCK IS KNOWN AS ONE OF THE MOST COLORFUL BIRDS IN THE ANIMAL KINGDOM. The beauty and unity of the colors in their plumage combined with their royal carriage are a visual testament to the elegance of the peacock. Even though the male is known for the beautiful fan of color, Kathleen's Peacock Ponshawl is my humble attempt to pay homage first to the beauty of my mother Kathleen, and next to the plumage of the female peacock. Reflect on the colorful, beautiful qualities of the mother figure in your life as you create your own version of Kathleen's Peacock.

Yarn

6 balls (100 yards each) Trendsetter Dolcino Ribbon in turquoise (MC)

2 balls (72 yards each) Trendsetter Joy in turquoise (A)

1 ball (72 yards) Trendsetter Joy in turquoise/white (B)

1 ball (202 yards) Ironstone Yarns Paris Nights in turquoise (C)

1 ball (145 yards) Trendsetter Aura in turquoise (D)

1 ball (72 yards) Trendsetter Metal Eyelash in turquoise (E)

1 hank (120 yards) Trendsetter Segue Ribbon in turquoise

Hook and Notions

15mm crochet hook

3 or 4 large buttons

Instructions

Foundation Chain: Using MC, chain 41.

Block 1: Holding MC and D together, start in second ch from hook and work 1 sc in each rem ch (40 sts). At end of row, ch 1 and turn work. Cont to work 1 sc in every st (40 sts) until piece measures 3" (8cm) from beg.

Block 2: Cut yarn D at end of row and tie on color C. Holding MC and C together, cont to work 1 sc in each rem st (40 sts). Ch 1 and turn work. Cont to work in sc for 4" (10cm). Piece measures 7" (18cm) from beg.

Block 3: At end of row, cut C and tie on A. Holding MC and A together, cont to work 1 sc in each st across all sts (40 sts) for 4" (10cm). Piece measures 11" (28cm) from beg.

Block 4: At end of row, cut A and join D. Holding D and MC together, work 1 sc in each st across all sts (40 sts). Cont in sc for 5" (13cm). Piece measures 16" (41cm) from beg.

Block 5: At end of row, cut D and tie on C. Holding MC and C together, cont in sc for 4" (10cm). Piece measures 20" (51cm) from beg.

Block 6: At end of row, cut C and tie on E. Holding MC and E together, cont in sc for 5" (13cm). Piece measures 25" (64cm) from beg.

Block 7: At end of row, cut E and tie on A. Holding MC and A together, cont in sc for 4" (10cm). Piece measures 29" (74cm).

Block 8: At end of row, cut A and tie on E. Holding MC and E together, cont in sc for 5"(13cm). Piece measures 34" (86cm) from beg.

Block 9: At end of row, cut E and tie on A. Holding MC and A together, cont in sc for 4"(10cm). Piece measures 38" (97cm) from beg.

Block 10: At end of row, cut A and tie on D. Holding MC and D together, cont in sc for 5" (13cm). Piece measures 43" (109cm) from beg.

Block 11: At end of row, cut D and tie on C. Holding MC and C together, cont in sc for 6"(15cm). Piece measures 49" (124cm) from beg.

Block 12: At end of row, cut C and tie on D. Holding MC and D together, cont in sc for 5"(13cm). Piece measures 54" (137cm) from beg.

Block 13: At end of row, cut D and tie on C. Holding MC and C together, cont in sc for 4" (13cm). Piece measures 58" (147cm) from beg.

End work by cutting yarn and pulling tails of MC and C through last st.

Finishing

Fold your ponshawl in half, bringing the 16" (41cm) sides together (see Diagram 2 on page 45). Sew on three or four buttons using a darning needle and heavy thread, spacing them evenly from the open end towards the fold. Leave about 12" (30cm) without buttons to create an opening for the head when the ponshawl is buttoned. There is no need for buttonholes. The stitch size is large enough to accommodate most buttons. If the stitches are too large for your buttons, you can sew or crochet around the opening to tighten it up. If you are adding fringe, unbutton the ponshawl and place fringe where desired on the open sides of the rectangle as shown in Diagram 2 on page 45.

DIAGRAM 1

BLOCK 1
3" (8cm) MC and D held together

BLOCK 2
4" (10cm) MC and C held together

BLOCK 3
4" (10cm) MC and A held together

BLOCK 4
5" (13cm) MC and D held together

BLOCK 5
4" (10cm) MC and C held together

BLOCK 6
5" (13cm) MC and E held together

BLOCK 7
4" (10cm) MC and A held together

BLOCK 8
5" (13cm) MC and E held together

BLOCK 9
4" (10cm) MC and A held together

BLOCK 10
5" (13cm) MC and D held together

BLOCK 11
6" (15cm) MC and C held together

BLOCK 12
5" (13cm) MC and D held together

BLOCK 13
4" (10cm) MC and C held together

16" (41cm)

DIAGRAM 2

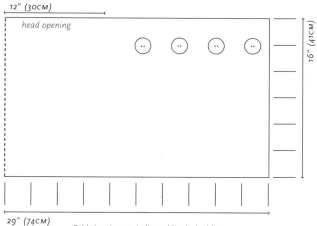

12" (30cm)

head opening

58" (147cm)

16" (41cm)

29" (74cm)

Fold the piece as indicated by dashed line.

Marsha's Corner

When your ponshawl is unbuttoned, it's a shawl. When buttoned, it can be turned at an angle and worn as a poncho. Place the buttons in front or back to wear it as a ruana (traditionally a large, open cape-like wrap where one side or both can be draped over the opposite shoulder). You might even unbutton one button and slide the ponshawl down so it drapes like a Sari across one shoulder. Slide the ponshawl down around your waist to create a skirt or swim cover-up.

The Grass Is Greener Ponshawl

As I sit on the porch looking at my yard, it doesn't take long for my gaze to wander to my neighbors' perfectly manicured lawns. Inevitably, my neighbors' grass is lusher, healthier, better groomed, and yes, you've guessed it, greener. If I can't have a perfect yard, I might as well wear a beautiful garment inspired by that ideal, right? In creating a poncho around a theme, I created a new look for the basic ponshawl pattern. Crocheted on a 17mm hook with multiple strands of yarn, one that has eyelash as a part of the fiber (Trendsetter Bugia), it is easy to achieve this grassy look. You may choose any kind of yarn in the green family. Here are some yarns I used: Trendsetter strander in Spruce Forest Green (color 8) carried with Plymouth Sunsette yarn in green, Trendsetter Bugia eyelash in green (color 15). Fringe the ponshawl with a shiny, wide ribbon yarn (such as Trendsetter Segue Ribbon in Mossy Pine [color 15]) to complete the look.

Is it a poncho? Is it a shawl? Is it a ruana? You decide. A ponshawl combines the style of a poncho, the ease of a shawl and the style of a ruana (see Marsha's Corner on page 45). Constructed from one large rectangle with strategically placed buttons, the ponshawl is a most versatile wardrobe essential.

Pride and Soy Ponshawl

Soy-based yarns are among the hot fibers of the new millennium. Pride and Soy is made using Soy Silk Oasis yarn as the base yarn (it is used throughout the project). Instead of using a monocrhomatic color theme, as in The Grass Is Greener, this ponshawl looks like it was inspired by a box of crayons. To make this wrap, crochet several strands of yarn of various textures and bright colors together with a 12mm hook. Here are some yarns I chose to strand with the soy yarn: Plymouth Salsa textural yarn in red/orange blend (color 6), Trendsetter Sunshine print yarn in orange blend (color 8) and Yang Yarn in orange multi (color 04). Tassel fringe made from a ladder yarn like Plymouth Odyssey provides the perfect accent. Perfect for wearing casually with jeans, Pride and Soy will be the pride and joy of your wardrobe.

Claudia's Hand Shrawl

■ ■ ■ WHEN I WAS SHOPPING AT A FIBER MARKET RECENTLY, I noticed a beautiful selection of hand-dyed yarns. The colors caught my attention from a distance, and I was drawn into the booth. As I touched the first, smooth strand, a merino wool, I was amazed at its softness. It was almost as soft as cashmere. Then I noticed that each merino wool had a companion bouclé. Right away I knew I wanted to create something beautiful with the yarn I was touching. That's when I met Claudia, who had dyed the fibers herself. She began her company, Claudia's Hand, as a way to pursue her passion and support herself. Claudia is an inspiration to me, and I am blessed to have met her and to have heard her story. This shrawl reflects the warmth of the woman who dyed these fibers just for me to use in a project for this book. I share this special treasure with you—from Claudia's Hand, through my hands, and into yours.

Yarn

500 yards Claudia's Hand Painted Yarns worsted merino in Bearded Iris (MC) or substitute any worsted weight smooth yarn

500 yards Claudia's Hand Painted Yarns boucle kid mohair/wool/nylon blend in Bearded Iris (A) or substitute any mohair boucle

2 balls (65 yards each) Trendsetter Coconut in Moss Lilac (B)

1 ball (72 yards) Trendsetter Joy in Gold (C)

1 ball (72 yards) Trendsetter Joy in Lilac (D)

Hooks

15mm (P or Q) crochet hook (smaller hook)

20mm crochet hook (larger hook)

Instructions (make 2)

FOUNDATION CHAIN: Using smaller hook and holding MC and A together, chain 51.

BLOCK 1: Holding MC and A together, start in second ch from hook and work 1 sc in each rem ch (50 sts). Ch 1 and turn work. Cont in sc for 2 rows.

BLOCK 2: At end of row, join color D. Holding MC, A and D together, switch to larger hook and cont to work 1 sc in each st (50 sts). Cont in sc for 2" (5cm). Piece measures 4" (10cm) from beg.

BLOCK 3: At end of row, cut yarn D. Holding MC and A together, cont in sc for 10" (25cm). Piece measures 14" (36cm) from beg.

BLOCK 4: At end of row, join color D. Holding MC, A and D together, cont in sc for 3" (8cm). Piece measures 17" (43cm) from beg.

BLOCK 5: At end of row, cut D. Holding MC and A together, cont in sc for 10" (25cm). Piece measures 27" (69cm) from beg.

BLOCK 6: At end of row, join color C. Holding MC, A and C together, cont in sc for 2" (5cm). Piece measures 29" (74cm) from beg.

BLOCK 7: At end of row, cut C. Holding MC and A together, cont in sc for 8" (20cm). Piece measures 37" (94cm) from beg.

BLOCK 8: Cut A and join in color B. Holding MC and B together, switch to smaller hook and cont in sc for 2 rows. Piece measures approx 40" (102cm) from beg.

Cut yarn, tie off and weave in all tails. Repeat for second rectangle.

Finishing

FOLD RECTANGLE LENGTHWISE
When the rectangle is finished, fold it in half lengthwise so that the 40" (102cm) sides match up, keeping right sides together.

CREATE ARMHOLES
Measure 8" to 9" (20cm to 23cm) along each 25" (64cm) edge down from the fold and mark with a stitch marker or scrap yarn of a different color. These are the openings for the armholes. Beginning at the marker, seam the remaining 16" to 17" (41cm to 43cm) of the short sides together (see Diagram 2, page 51). Turn garment to right side.

For a shorter length from the shoulder down the back, decrease the 25" (64cm) measurement by decreasing the number of chains in the foundation chain. See the information on gauge in the Useful Information section, page 122, for more information on adjusting a pattern.

DIAGRAM 1
[MAKE 2]

BLOCK 1
2 rows MC and A held together

BLOCK 2
2" (5cm) MC, A and D held together

BLOCK 3
10" (25cm) MC and A held together

BLOCK 4
3" (8cm) MC, A and D held together

BLOCK 5
10" (25cm) MC and A held together

BLOCK 6
2" (5cm) MC, A and C held together

BLOCK 7
8" (20cm) MC and A held together

BLOCK 8
2 rows MC and B held together

40" (102CM)

25" (64CM)

DIAGRAM 2

8" TO 9" (20CM TO 23CM)

16" TO 17" (41CM TO 43CM)

arm hole

arm hole

join with single crochet seam

join with single crochet seam

Fold the piece as indicated by dashed lines, and seam pieces together as indicated by all dotted lines.

Ocean Mist Shrawl

Mohair yarn (in this case, Plymouth Yarn Outback Mohair in pale gray-green blend [color 801]) in colors reminiscent of ocean waves crocheted on a large 17mm hook makes this shrawl as light as an ocean mist. Notice how a non-bouclé mohair used by itself creates a lighter version of Claudia's Hand. This is a very easy project that can be completed in just a few hours.

A shrawl combines the style of a shrug with the ease and warmth of a shawl. "Sleeves" help transform this rectangle into a shawl that stays on your shoulders. Accent it with a vintage pin or a large button. Both of these shrawls can be made following the same pattern as for Claudia's Hand Shrawl (pages 50–51).

Orange You Glad Shrawl

I refer to this project as a "stash buster." It starts with about 500 yards of a chunky cotton-blend yarn. Use the cotton alone, or strand it with coordinating colors from your stash. I used Gedifra Luisa in orange, but since this yarn is discontinued, any bulky weight cotton blend in an orange color will do. A 19mm hook opens up the stitches to form the perfect summer covering. This project, unlike Ocean Mist, is worked in one seamless piece as a 44" x 30" (112cm x 76cm) rectangle. Orange you glad there's no seaming? Simply fold it in half and follow the general instructions for creating a shrawl, as illustrated on pages 50–51).

Painter's Palette Poncho

■ ■ ■ A PAINTER CREATES HER OWN PALETTE OF COLOR, drawn from the inspiration she receives from the subject she is painting. Inspiration is a key link to creative expression, in fiberwork as well as in painting. This poncho, while basic in shape, is a challenging exercise in yarn selection, color and textural harmony. It is my way of translating a painter's palette into wearable art. The process for this piece begins with selecting a palette or theme and then digging into your yarn stash. Your task is to find colors and textures that fit your theme. Don't be afraid to experiment with color and texture. The finished poncho should look like an artist's palette as the fibers come together for the finished garment. Need help choosing yarns? Get assistance from your local yarn shop or order a premade kit.

Yarn

900 yards of assorted fibers of the same gauge

1 hank (100 yards) hand-dyed ribbon yarn for fringe

Hook

12mm crochet hook

Instructions

FOUNDATION CHAIN: Chain 101 with any yarn. You may have to adjust the number of stitches to achieve the measurements given. See the Useful Information section, page 122, for specific information about gauge.

REMAINDER: Starting in second ch from hook, work 1 sc in each of the rem ch (100 sts). Ch 1 and turn work. Cont to work 1 sc in each st across all sts until piece measures 25" (64cm) from beg. (The finished rectangle will measure 60" x 25" [152cm x 64cm].) Change yarns as one runs out or where desired. There is no special formula—it's even OK to change yarns in the middle of a row. You may tie your yarns together and leave the tails showing for a different design effect.

Cut yarn, tie off and weave in all tails (or leave them sticking out, as desired).

Finishing

Fold the finished rectangle in half, matching up the 25" (64cm) sides (see Diagram 1 on page 57). Join one of the 30" (76cm) sides (created by the fold) together from the open end toward the fold, leaving 9" to 12" (23cm to 30cm) open for the head. The remaining 30" (76cm) side should be left open—it will become one of the bottom edges of the poncho (see Diagram 2 on page 57). When worn, the poncho is an offset diamond shape.

DIAGRAM 1

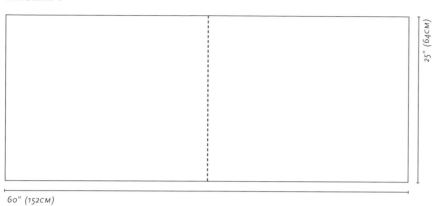

25" (64CM)

60" (152CM)

DIAGRAM 2

9" TO 12" (23CM TO 30CM)

18" TO 21" (46CM TO 53CM)

head opening

25" (64CM)

30" (76CM)

*Fold the piece as indicated by dashed lines,
and seam pieces together as indicated by all dotted lines.*

Miter Square Shrawl

■ ■ ■ THE MITER SQUARE IS A SIMPLE WAY TO CREATE COMPLEX DESIGNS. It starts with a simple shape (the square) and uses it as a building block for creative design. Miter squares can be combined in a number of ways to form intricate pathways of color and texture. Miter squares can be joined by crocheting the squares together to form strips, as in this colorful shrawl. While there are methods for joining miter squares as you go, making the squares first and seaming them together at the end is a bit easier for beginners.

Yarn

1500 yards knitting worsted (shrawl as pictured was done using 14 balls of Baruffa Merino Otto)

assortment of novelty yarns, such as eyelash and fur (optional)

Hook

6.5mm (K, US 10½) crochet hook

Instructions

MAKE 88 SQUARES

You may use any combinations of yarn you like in each square.

FOUNDATION CHAIN: Chain 25 with worsted weight yarn.

Row 1: Starting in second ch from hook, work 1 sc in each of the next 11 ch, sk 2 sts, work 1 sc in rem 11 ch. Ch 1 and turn.

Row 2: Work 1 sc in each of the next 10 sts, sk 2 sts, work 1 sc in rem 10 sts. Ch 1 and turn.

Row 3: Work 1 sc in each of the next 9 sts, sk 2 sts, work 1 sc in rem 9 sts. Ch 1 and turn.

Rows 4–10: Decrease the number of single crochet stitches on either side of the 2 skipped stitches by 1 each time you finish a row. For example, for row 4 you work 1 sc in each of the first 8 sts, sk 2, work 1 sc in rem 8 sts. Keep decreasing each row as established. Always ch 1 at the end of each row before turning work.

FINAL ROW: For your final row, work 1 sc, sk 2 sts, work 1 sc in rem st. Ch 1, cut yarn and pull tail through to secure.

Finishing

JOIN SQUARES TO CREATE RECTANGLE

When you have finished all of the squares, lay them out on a flat surface and arrange them 11 across and 8 high. Move the squares around until you arrive at an arrangement you like. Join columns of 8 squares together with single crochet seams. Repeat until you have 11 strips with 8 squares each. Join the strips together along their long sides with a single crochet seam to create a large retangle, about 40" x 26" (102cm x 66cm). (See Diagram 1 on page 61.) You can adjust the size of the shrawl by increasing or decreasing the total number of squares or strips.

CREATE SHRAWL

When the strips are joined together, fold the rectangle in half lengthwise with right sides facing, matching up the long sides. Keeping right sides together, measure 8" to 9" (20cm to 23cm) down from the fold on both sides and place a marker. These are the openings for the armholes. Join the short sides of the rectangle together with a single crochet seam from each marker to the open edge of the rectangle (see Diagram 2, page 61). To finish the shrawl, work one or two rows of single crochet edging around the entire shrawl in eyelash or another textural yarn.

DIAGRAM 1

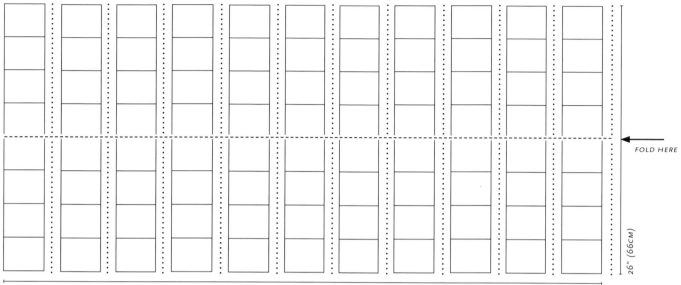

FOLD HERE

26" (66CM)

40" (102CM)

DIAGRAM 2

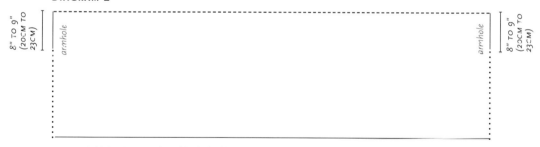

8" TO 9" (20CM TO 23CM)

armhole

armhole

8" TO 9" (20CM TO 23CM)

Fold the piece as indicated by dashed lines, and seam pieces together as indicated by all dotted lines.

ACCESSORIES

■■■ ACCESSORY IS THE MOTHER OF INVENTION...isn't that how the saying goes? At any rate, no wardrobe would be complete without a few key accent pieces. Unique blends of color and texture add elegance and style to everything from caps and bags to slippers and totes. In this section, you'll also find easy projects for baby, like the Bouncing Baby Boy Cap (it looks just as cute on a tiny girl!). Practice the technique for making the "That's My Baby" Booties, and then use the same technique to make Vallarie's Royal Slippers—you'll never have cold feet again! You might also try your hand at crocheting a bag, big or small—there's something here for every occasion.

Bouncing Baby Boy
cardigan & cap

■■■ I HAVE TWO GROWN CHILDREN, BOTH BOYS. This cap and cardigan set reminds me of my boys when they were babies. Remembering slobbery kisses and gentle hugs, I can almost see my chubby Martin, and my precious preemie, Michael, wearing this matching hat and sweater. I can almost hear the teasing and crying of two boys in "heated debate." I can just about feel the pain of skinned knees and bumped heads. I still smile when I think about high school and college graduations. Then reality brings me back. Both of my sons are grown up, and I don't have any grandchildren (yet). For me, the Bouncing Baby Boy set is more than mere clothing, it is memories of days gone by, and reflections of what the future may bring.

Yarn

8 balls (120 yards each) Cascade Pearls thick and thin cotton yarn in blue (A) *use 2 balls for the cap and 6 for the cardigan*

3 balls (99 yards each) Filatura di Crosa Casablanca flag strander yarn in blue (B) *use 1 ball for the cap and 2 for the cardigan*

Hooks and Notions

9mm (M, N US 13) crochet hook

6.5mm (K, US 10½) hook (for Bouncing Baby Boy Cardigan)

3 buttons for cardigan

cardigan

Instructions

BACK

FOUNDATION CHAIN: Holding 2 strands of yarn A together, ch 26.

REMAINDER: Starting in second ch from hook, work 1 sc in each of the rem ch (25 sts). Ch 1 and turn. Cont to work 1 sc in each ch (25 sts) until piece measures 10" (25cm) from beg. Cut yarn and tie off.

FRONT (MAKE 2)

FOUNDATION CHAIN: Holding 2 strands of yarn A together, ch 13.

REMAINDER: Starting in second ch from hook, work 1 sc in each of the rem ch (12 sts). Ch 1 and turn. Cont to work 1 sc in each st (12 sts) until piece measures 10" (25cm) from beg. Cut yarn and tie off.

SLEEVES (MAKE 2)

FOUNDATION CHAIN: Holding 2 strands of yarn A together, chain 21 with the 6.5mm hook.

ROWS 1 AND 2: Starting in second ch from hook, work 1 sc in each of the rem ch (20 sts). Ch 1 and turn.

REMAINDER: Switch to the 9mm hook and cont to work 1 sc in each st (20 sts) until piece measures 10" (25cm) from beg. Cut yarn and tie off.

Finishing

PLACE MARKERS FOR ARMHOLES AND LAPELS

Measure 4" to 5" (10cm to 13cm) from the top of the back down each side and place a safety pin or marker for the armhole openings. Repeat for the front panels. Place a marker on each front panel about 2" (5cm) from the edge opposite the armhole edge for the lapel.

SEAM SHOULDERS

Pin the front panels to the back panel with right sides facing, matching up the edges of the front panels with the edges of the back panel. Seam the tops of the front and back together with a single crochet seam to create the shoulder seams. Leave the final 2" (5cm) on each panel open for the lapels (see Diagram 1 below).

ATTACH SLEEVES

Place a marker at the top center of each sleeve. With right sides facing, pin the center of each sleeve to the center of each shoulder seam. Seam the sleeves to the body of the jacket with a single crochet seam (see Diagram 1 below).

SEAM SIDES AND SLEEVES

Pin the sides together with right sides facing and join them with a single crochet seam using yarn A. Work from start of sleeve to the underarm, then down the side (see Diagram 2 below).

ADD BUTTONS

Add buttons to the left side of cardigan, sewing them on with needle and thread.

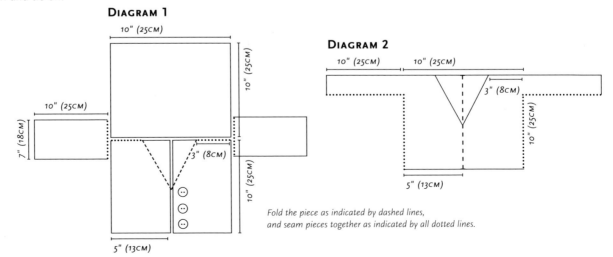

DIAGRAM 1

10" (25CM)

10" (25CM)

10" (25CM)

7" (18CM)

3" (8CM)

10" (25CM)

5" (13CM)

DIAGRAM 2

10" (25CM) 10" (25CM)

3" (8CM)

10" (25CM)

5" (13CM)

*Fold the piece as indicated by dashed lines,
and seam pieces together as indicated by all dotted lines.*

cap

Instructions

FOUNDATION CHAIN: Holding 2 strands of yarn A together, chain 26.

REMAINDER: Starting in second ch from hook, work 1 sc in each of the rem 25 ch. Ch 1 and turn work. Cont to work 1 sc in each ch (25 sts) until piece measures 10" (25cm) from beg. Cut yarn and tie off.

Finishing

SEAM SIDES OF HAT TOGETHER
Fold hat in half and seam both sides with a single crochet seam (see Diagrams 1 and 2, below). Leave the bottom open.

ADD TASSEL FRINGE

Measure 12 6" (15cm) strands of yarn A and six 6" (15cm) strands of yarn B for the tassel fringe at the corners of the hat. Using a tapestry needle or hook, attach six strands of yarn A and three strands of yarn B as tassel fringe to each top corner of hat (see Crochet 101, pages 24–26 for detailed instructions on attaching tassels).

DIAGRAM 1

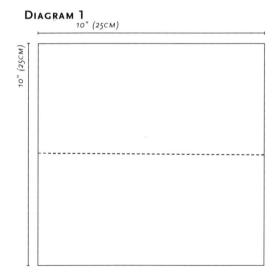

10" (25CM)

10" (25CM)

DIAGRAM 2

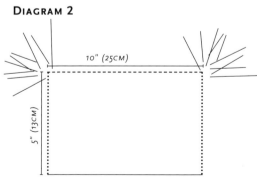

10" (25CM)

5" (13CM)

Fold the piece as indicated by dashed lines, and seam pieces together as indicated by all dotted lines.

Vickie's Bad Hair Day Hat

■ ■ ■ WE'VE ALL HAD A BAD HAIR DAY OR TWO IN OUR TIME. For some of us, our hair looks like it's about to fly off on its own. Or maybe our head looks like it has grown an extra appendage that just happens to be our hair. Or, perhaps your hair looks like it needs to be combed or brushed, even when you just finished combing or brushing it. Whatever the reason, bad hair can ruin your day if you let it. My good friend Vickie believes that you need to go with the flow. When life gives you lemons, make lemonade. When you have a bad hair day, wear a hat.

Yarn

3 balls (80 yards/ball) Tahki Yarns Poppy, color 002 (A)

3 balls (60 yards/ball) di.ve Orientale, color 34325 (B)

Hook

9mm (M, N US 13) crochet hook

Instructions

The instructions below are for a small adult hat. See the sizing chart for instructions on adjusting size.

FOUNDATION CHAIN: Holding yarns A and B together, ch 47(52, 55).

REMAINDER: Starting in second ch from hook, work 1 sc in each rem ch (46 sts). At end of row, ch 1 and turn work. Cont to work 1 sc in each st (45 sts) until piece measures 10" (25cm) from beg.

Finishing

Fold the cap in half and seam the side opposite the fold with a single crochet seam, as indicated in Diagram 1 on page 71 (see Crochet 101, page 29, for detailed instructions for making single crochet seams). After seaming the side, you will have a tube-like piece of fabric, open at either end. For flat shaping (see Diagram 3 on page 71), seam the top of the hat with a single crochet seam. For more shaping, pinch the top of the hat together so it resembles a four-leaf clover and sew the sides of the "star" together (see Diagram 2 on page 71).

SIZING CHART

To determine the proper size for your cap, simply measure the circumference of your head with a measuring tape. Most yarns have a little bit of give, so a snug fit is best.

General guidelines for adult hat sizes are as follows:

Small: 20" to 21" (50cm to 53cm)

Medium: 22" (56cm)

Large: 23" to 24" (58cm to 61cm)

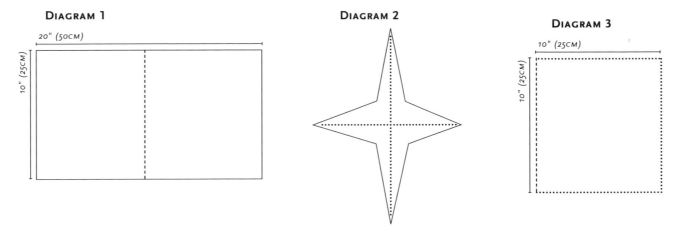

DIAGRAM 1

20" (50CM)

10" (25CM)

DIAGRAM 2

DIAGRAM 3

10" (25CM)

10" (25CM)

Fold the piece as indicated by dashed lines, and seam pieces together as indicated by all dotted lines.

Miriam's Savvy Chenille Hat

For a different look, follow the instructions on page 70, including seaming the side opposite the fold. Take a 10" (25cm) length of ribbon or a piece of the yarn used to make the hat and tie a bow around the hat, about 2" (5cm) down from the top of the hat. The hat will appear to be shaped with sloping sides and a square of fabric at the top. Note: This hat is made from a very bulky chenille (Trendsetter Savvy yarn in Bright Black/Multi [color 76]), so you'll need to adjust the number of stitches accordingly (see Useful Information, page 122 for information on how to adjust gauge).

"That's My Baby" Booties

■■■ THESE TINY CREATIONS ARE SO CUTE. I am providing two variations of the essential accessory for any baby's wardrobe. Try combining smooth, dyed yarns with eyelash or fur fibers for that special touch. Since this project doesn't use much yarn, it's the perfect opportunity to splurge on fine fibers like silk or cashmere. You can also coordinate an ensemble with a matching cap and sweater. There are two versions of this project, and one set of booties even has a matching cardigan. Whatever you decide, the "That's My Baby" Booties are a timeless project, perfect for the beginning crocheter.

Yarn

1 ball (110 yards) Adriafil Fluo in Baby Blue Multi (color 23) (A)

1 ball (88 yards) Adriafil Puff in Baby Blue Multi (color 43) (B)

1 ball (82 yards) Debbie Bliss Cashmerino Super Chunky in Olive Green (crochet 1 strand), or 1 ball Cascade Pearls in Sky Blue (color 2477) (crochet as 2 strands)

Hook

9mm (M, N US 13) crochet hook

Instructions (make 2)

These simple baby booties are made by cheating the square. The booties are basically squares, but the curved toe is created by single crocheting several stitches together. Before you begin the baby booties, decide what size you want the bootie to be (newborn, 9 months, or 18 months). Instructions given are for a newborn. The remaining sizes follow in parentheses.

FOUNDATION CHAIN: Holding yarns A and B together, ch 19 (22, 25).

SECTION 1: Starting in second ch from hook, work 1 sc in each of the rem ch (18 [21, 24]) sts. Cont to work 1 sc in each st until piece measures 2½" (6cm) from beg.

SECTION 2: On next row, work 1 sc across the next 6 (7, 8) sts. Yarn over and draw up a loop as if to sc, but leave the loop on the hook. Repeat until there are 6 (7, 8) loops on the hook. Yarn over and pull all the loops off the hook as if making a regular sc st (you will have one loop on hook now). Work 1 sc in each rem st (6 [7, 8] sts).

SECTION 3: Work 1 sc across rem sts (12 [14, 16] sts) for 2 to 3 more rows. End work by cutting the tail and pulling it through the final loop.

Finishing

Each bootie should look like a fat L shape. Fold the bootie in half, matching up the two legs of the L. The toe part of the bootie is slightly rounded. Beginning at the toe, join the edges together with a single crochet seam. Remember to leave an opening at the top of the bootie. Cut yarn and pull tail through loop to secure. Weave in all tails. If desired, work one row of single crochet around the bootie opening. Repeat to make the second bootie.

DIAGRAM 1

DIAGRAM 2

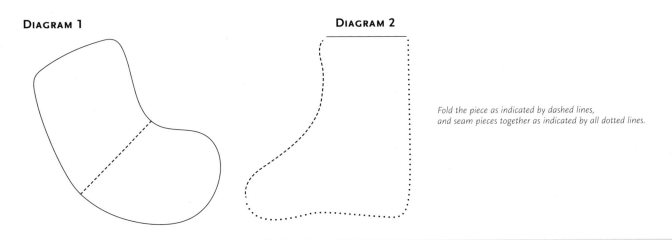

Fold the piece as indicated by dashed lines, and seam pieces together as indicated by all dotted lines.

Marsha's Corner

A crocheter's "hand" is the way she holds the hook, the way she holds the yarn, the way she forms her stitches, etc. It can be affected by varying circumstances on any given day. To help maintain symmetry when making booties or slippers, try to allow time to make two. In most cases, booties can be made in about an hour, and you can seam them later.

Green Peas and Grape Juice
Baby Sweater and Booties

This baby set won't make strained peas taste any better, but if your bundle of joy is wearing this cashmere blend, at least she'll look good while she's being fed. Use the same techniques as for making the "That's My Baby" Booties. Splurge on a fine cashmere yarn (such as Cashmerino super chunky in Hunter Green [color 07] stranded with Crystal Palace Fizz in Cool Jazz [color 7123]) to create this cute set for baby. (Use the pattern on page 67 to make the cardigan.)

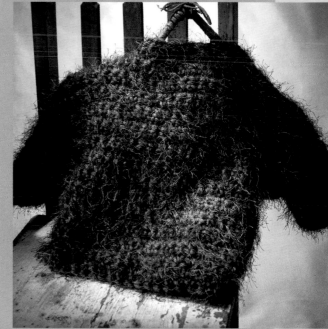

Vallarie's Royal Slippers

■ ■ ■ VALLARIE IS MY FIRST COUSIN. We grew up like sisters. However, our internal thermostats are on opposite ends of the spectrum. I am always very hot, and Vallarie is always cold. She can wrap up in a blanket all year round. She is probably the last person in Ohio to turn on the air-conditioning in summer, and the first person to need heat in winter. Vallarie loves to put on knee socks, wrap herself in one of my body drapes, curl up by the fireplace and drink a cup of green tea from a fine china cup. She looks very regal wrapped in this manner. These slippers were designed to provide royal warmth and comfort for all the Vallaries with cold feet.

Yarn
3 balls Aurora (49 yards each), color Blue/Purple (A)
2 balls Trendsetter (80 yards each) eyelash, color 31 or dark purple (B)

Hooks
9mm (M, N US 13) crochet hook
10mm (P US 15) crochet hook

Instructions (make 2)

One size fits most for this slipper. (Note Marsha's Corner for sizing slippers.) Vallarie's Royal Slippers are made just like the "That's My Baby" Booties, but on a larger scale.

FOUNDATION CHAIN: Holding yarns A and B together, use a 9mm hook to ch 40.

SECTION 1: Starting in second ch from hook, work 1 sc in each rem ch (39 sts). Ch 1 and turn work. Cont to work 1 sc in each st (39 sts) until piece measures 5" (13cm) from beg.

SECTION 2: On the next row, work 1 sc across 1/3 of the stitches (13 sts). Draw up a loop as if to sc, but leave the loop on the hook as you work the next 1/3 of the sts (13 sts). You will have 13 sts on your hook. Yarn over and pull all the loops off as if working 1 sc (you will have one loop on the hook now). Work 1 sc in each rem st (13 sts).

SECTION 3: Using a 9mm hook, work 1 sc across rem sts (26 sts) for 2 to 3 more rows. Cut yarn and tie off to end.

Finishing

Each slipper should look like a fat L shape. Fold the slipper in half, matching up the two legs of the L. The toe part of the slipper will look slightly rounded. Beginning at the toe, join the edges together with a single crochet seam. Remember to leave an opening at the top of the slipper. Cut yarn and pull tail through loop to secure. Weave in all tails. If desired, work one row of single crochet around the slipper opening. Repeat to make the second slipper.

DIAGRAM 1

Fold the piece as indicated by dashed lines, and seam pieces together as indicated by all dotted lines.

DIAGRAM 2

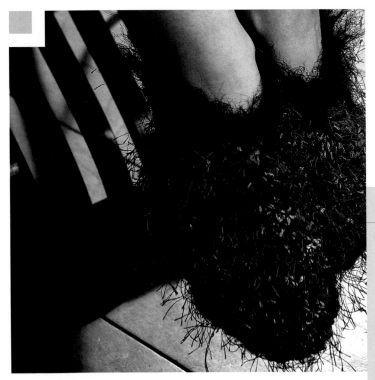

Marsha's Corner

While these slippers are pretty much one size fits all, you can get a more precise fit by measuring your foot. If you are making the adult version, measure the foot from toe to heel. Chain long enough to fit this measurement, making sure that the number is divisible by three. It is better to make the slipper slightly smaller than needed as the slipper will stretch with wear. If you'd like to make your slippers no-slip, there are products available at your local craft store that you can apply to the bottom of the slipper to make it less slick.

Pastel Paradise Slippers

Another way to make slippers is to simply
crochet a square. Form a slipper by folding
the square in half lengthwise. Join the edges
of the slipper with a single crochet seam at
each end of the rectangle. Single crochet across
3" to 4" (8cm to 10cm) at the top edge of the
bootie, leaving several inches open for the foot.
To make these slippers, I used Nashua Knits
Creative Focus worsted weight yarn in the pastel
pink colorway. Single crochet around the top of
the slipper with an eyelash or furry yarn to form
the opening for the foot.

3" to 4" (8cm to 10cm)

slipper opening

heel

toe

*Fold the piece as indicated by dashed lines,
and seam pieces together as indicated by all dotted lines.*

Jessica-Loves-Chocolate Purse

■ ■ ■ My editor, Jessica, could eat chocolate for breakfast, lunch and dinner. From exquisite chocolate truffles to M&Ms in a pinch, no chocolate goes unappreciated by Jessica. I, on the other hand, am one of the few people in the world who is not that crazy about chocolate. While I eat it on occasion, it is not my favorite thing. Even to me, however, this simple rectangular purse looks almost good enough to eat. It delights Jessica, and it should inspire any chocoholic crocheter.

Yarn

Use odds and ends of various yarns from your stash. The list below reflects odds and ends from my stash.

2 balls (120 yards each) Rowan Cotton Glace in mocha (A)

2 balls (120 yards each) Rowan Cotton Glace in black (B)

1 ball (72 yards) Trendsetter eyelash in brown (C)

1 ball (100 yards) Crystal Palace Squiggle Print in woodgrain (D)

1 ball (148 yards) Trendsetter Aura in brown tones (E)

1 ball (165 yards) Plymouth Eros in brown tones (F)

1 ball (120 yards) Crystal Palace Fizz in woodgrain (G)

1 ball (187 yards) Plymouth 24K in brown tones (H)

1 ball (71 yards) On Line Allegro in earth tones (I)

Hook and Notions

10mm (P US 15)crochet hook

1 large button or bead

Instructions

Since this purse is made from scrap yarns, you can have some creative fun by deviating from the listed materials. Try using your choice of the following: 200 yards of worsted weight yarn in your favorite chocolate color (Cascade 220, Nashua Knits Creative Focus, Lion Brand, etc.) and 200 yards of novelty strander of your choice. Think of colors found in your favorite chocolate concoction. This project is made in strips that are joined together later. You may combine square and rectangle shapes to create one piece of square fabric that measures approximately 9" x 9" (23cm x 23cm). Or you may choose to make just one large 9" x 9" (23cm x 23cm) square. Those with more conservative taste may choose to create this bag with beautiful smooth fibers and omit the stranders.

Purse front and back

[STRIP ONE]

FOUNDATION CHAIN: Holding yarns A and D together, ch 10.

BLOCK 1: Starting in second ch from hook, work 1 sc in each rem ch (9 sts). Ch 1 and turn work. Cont to work 1 sc in each st until piece measures 4½" (12cm) from beg. Block 2: Cut yarn D and cont with yarn A alone, working 1 sc in every st (9 sts) until strip measures 9" (23cm) from beg. Cut yarn and tie off.

[STRIP TWO]

FOUNDATION CHAIN: Holding yarns A and F together, ch 10.

BLOCK 1: Starting in second ch from hook, work 1 sc in each rem ch (9 sts). Cont to work 1 sc in every st (9 sts) until piece measures 4½" (12cm) from beg.

BLOCK 2: Cut yarn D and cont with yarn A alone, working 1 sc in every st (9 sts) until piece measures 9" (23cm) from beg. Cut yarn and tie off.

[STRIP THREE]

FOUNDATION CHAIN: With yarn I, ch 10

BLOCK 1: Starting in second ch from hook, work 1 sc in each rem ch (9 sts). Cont to work 1 sc in every st (9 sts) until piece measures 4½" (12cm) from beg.

BLOCK 2: Cut yarn I and cont with yarns B and F held together, working 1 sc in every st (9 sts) until piece measures 9" (23cm) from beg. Cut yarn and tie off.

Purse flap

Make one miter square with the color or colors of your choice. See Crochet 101 (page 31) for instructions on the miter square.

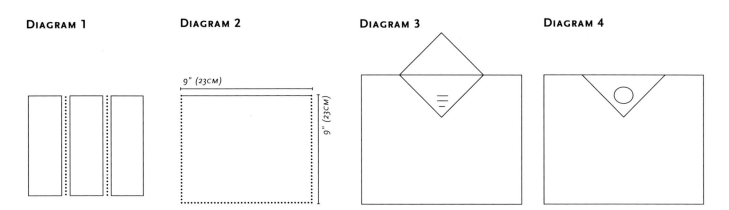

DIAGRAM 1   **DIAGRAM 2**   **DIAGRAM 3**   **DIAGRAM 4**

9" (23CM)   9" (23CM)

Fold the piece as indicated by dashed lines, and seam pieces together as indicated by all dotted lines.

Finishing

SEAM PIECES TOGETHER

To construct the purse, seam each set of three strips together with a single crochet seam, as shown in Diagram 1 on page 82. Place the purse front and back on top of each other with right sides facing and seam the sides together with a single crochet seam. Join the bottom edge of the purse with a single crochet seam as well. Leave the top of the purse open (see Diagram 2 on page 82).

CREATE BORDER AT TOP OF PURSE

Starting at a seam, use 1 strand of A and 1 strand of G held together to work two rows of single crochet around the upper edge of the purse. (Be careful not to crochet the top of the purse closed. Don't laugh, this has happened—I won't mention any names.)

ATTACH MITER SQUARE FLAP

Turn the miter square on point (so it looks like a diamond) and center one point at the center back of the purse. Attach the miter point to the purse at center back with a darning needle and yarn (see Diagram 3 on page 82). Attach a large button to the center front of the purse with needle and thread. The miter square forms a flap closure. The button fits into spaces in the crocheted fabric of the miter square (see Diagram 4 on page 82).

Yoruba Handbag

Inspired by the creativity of the Yoruba, the largest ethnic group in Africa, the unique colors, textures and fibers in this bag reflect the philosophy of a well-known Yoruba sculptor who said, "Each man's work is different." The irregular shape with its attention to detail further enhances the appeal of this bag. Use a 9mm (M, N US 13) hook and a selection of worsted weight yarns, and throw in a few stranders just for fun. To achieve the unique shape, crochet the last few inches across only half of your stitches. Use a miter square or crochet a small rectangle for the flap. When turned on point, the purse has a V or a heart shape. Follow the instructions on page 82 for attaching the flap and button and your purse is ready as a clutch. You can also make a shoulder strap by working single crochet across three stitches to the length you desire. Attach the strap to the sides and your bag is done.

This is truly a stash buster project. You may literally use any yarns in any combinations that you have. For example, some yarns I used are: Brown Sheep Lamb's Pride worsted, Nashua Knits Creative Focus worsted, Cascade 220, eyelash, Joy or any textural strander you find in the yarn shop in a color that contrasts or complements what you have in your stash.

Let's-Go-Shopping Tote

■■■ SHOPPING RANKS VERY HIGH ON MY LIST OF FAVORITE THINGS TO DO. Shopping for yarn is a double pleasure. The Let's-Go-Shopping Tote combines three of my passions: shopping, yarn and food. This tote is a shopper's dream. It is roomy and durable with fashion panache. It is made of wool and can be created in an endless palette of colors. I chose the colors for this project because they remind me of eggplant and sage (yes, I was thinking about food when I searched for just the right yarn for this project). This tote could be felted or lined for added strength and flair. It can even be used as a project bag or to hold an array of yarns. Make this tote, and then...let's go shopping!

Yarn

4 skeins (190 yards each) Lamb's Pride worsted in Clematis (A)

1 ball (72 yards) Plymouth Odyssey Glitz in Purple Tones (color 922) (B)

1 skein (190 yards) Lamb's Pride worsted in Oregano (C)

1 ball (72 yards) Trendsetter Papi in Purple (C)

Hook

9mm (M, N US 13) crochet hook

Instructions

Body (make 2)

Foundation Chain: Holding yarns A and B together, ch 45.

Section 1: Starting in second ch from hook, work 1 sc in each rem ch (44 sts). Ch 1 and turn work. Cont to work 1 sc in each st (44 sts) until piece measures 3" (8cm) from beg.

Section 2: Cut yarn B and, holding 2 strands of yarn A together, cont to work 1 sc in each st (44 sts) until piece measures 12" (31cm) from beg.

Section 3: Cut 1 strand of yarn A and join in 1 strand of yarn B. Work 1 sc in every st for 4 rows holding yarns A and B together. Ch 1 and turn at the end of each row.

Section 4: Cut yarn B and, using 2 strands of yarn A, cont to work 1 sc in every st (44 sts) until piece measures 16" (41cm) from beg.

Section 5: Cut yarn A and, using 2 strands of yarn B and 1 strand of yarn C held together, cont to work 1 sc in every st (44 sts) until piece measures 19" (48cm) from beg. Cut yarn and tie off.

Straps (make 2)

Foundation Chain: Holding yarns A and B together, ch 6.

Following and all subsequent rows: Starting in second ch from hook, work 1 sc in the rem 5 ch. Cont to work 1 sc in every st (5 sts) until piece measures 18" (46cm) from beg.

Finishing

Join Squares to Create Body of Tote

With right sides facing, seam the sides of the tote body together with a single crochet seam (see Diagram 1, page 87). As you seam, try to match the seam yarn with the striping in the body of the tote. Seam the bottom of the tote as well. Turn the tote right side out.

Attach Straps to Tote

Pin one end of each strap to each side of the tote, centering the straps so the tote will hang properly when carried. Attach the straps to the tote with yarn and tapestry needle or with a sewing machine (see Diagram 2, page 87). Your tote is complete.

Diagram 1

18" (46CM)

18" (46CM)

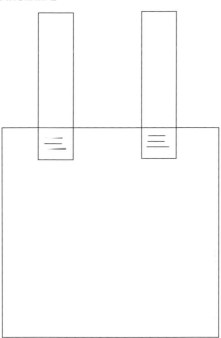

Diagram 2

Fold the piece as indicated by dashed lines,
and seam pieces together as indicated by all dotted lines.

Marsha's Corner

Once your tote is complete, use it as is, felt it, or add a lining.
You may also shorten the straps and make them wider, or
alter the size of the tote itself to suit your needs.

SHELLS, CARDIGANS
& JACKETS

■■■ THE PROJECTS IN THIS CHAPTER DEMONSTRATE THAT WITH A
LITTLE IMAGINATION, the basic square or rectangle is transformed into fashion-savvy,
contemporary garments. We will start with two squares, add a few beads and embellishments,
and the result is a "slight"-sleeved shell that is both unique and fashionable. Next, taking
inspiration from stained glass, we will create a beautiful short-sleeved cardigan. We can then
apply these techniques to combine squares and rectangles to form stunning jackets. Use the
yarns suggested for these projects or have fun substituting yarns and fibers from your stash.
Whatever you decide, be prepared to crochet eye-catching, spectacular pieces.

Deep Blue Sea
beaded shell

■ ■ ■ PERFECT TO WEAR WITH JEANS OR UNDER THAT SPECIAL SUIT, the Deep Blue Sea shell shows that a little beading goes a long way. The yarn used for this project was selected for its transitioning shades of blue. The variance in color mimics the subtle waves of a calm sea. The glass beads are placed strategically to imitate water bubbles and to add flair and detail. Don't worry, though, the "waves" created by single crochet embellishment on top of the finished piece won't make you seasick. Dive right into this fun project and "sea" for yourself.

Yarn

1 hank (124 yards) Intermezzo chunky mercerized cotton in sea blue (A)

8 spools (75 yards) Mango Moon ribbon in blue tones (B)

several yards Plymouth Yarn Color Lash (eyelash yarn) in turquoise

1 ball (70 yards) Schachenmayr Nomotta Laisa metallic yarn in Royal Blue

Hooks and Notions

6.5mm (K US 10½) crochet hook

very small crochet hook to fit through beads and paillettes

25 glass beads (hole should be large enough to insert a small crochet hook)

8 paillettes

Instructions

The cotton yarn is slightly heavier than the ribbon yarn, which adds a little weight to the bottom of the shell and gives the illusion of shaping. One size fits most. The finished measurements are approx 20" wide x 22" long (50cm x 56cm). To make the shell wider, add more stitches to your starting chain. To make the shell longer, work more rows.

Paillettes and beads are added as a border on the front of the shell to imitate waves and surf. Additional beads are attached randomly onto the top front and the back of the shell. You may choose to place the beads in any configuration you choose.

Optional: The Laisa yarn is used as a single crochet embellishment at the base of the front of the shell. It is also stranded with the cotton. A small amount of eyelash is also used for two rows in the front.

BACK

FOUNDATION CHAIN: Ch 56 with yarn A (held together with Laisa, if desired).

SECTION 1: Starting in second ch from hook, work 1 sc in each rem ch (55 sts). Ch 1 and turn work. Cont to work 1 sc in every st (55 sts) until piece measures 3½" (9cm) from beg.

SECTION 2: Switch to yarn B and cont to work 1 sc in every st (55 sts) until piece measures 22" (56cm) from beg (or desired length). As you crochet, attach 6 beads randomly across the back. I placed beads at 5" (13cm), 7" (18cm), 10" (25cm), 13" (33cm), 15" (38cm) and 17" (43cm). Cut yarn and tie off.

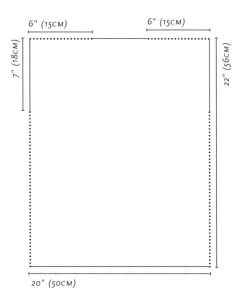

Seam pieces together as indicated by dotted lines.

Front

FOUNDATION CHAIN: Ch 56 with yarn A (held together with Laisa, if desired).

SECTION 1: Starting in second ch from hook, work 1 sc in every rem ch (55 sts). Ch 1 and turn work. Cont to work 1 sc in every st for 2 rows.

SECTION 2: Switch to yarn B and work 1 sc in every st (55 sts) for 2 rows.

SECTION 3: Work 1 sc in each of the next 8 sts, switch to the smaller hook and attach a paillette (see Crochet 101, pages 20–21). Cont to work 1 sc in every st, adding a paillette every 7 sts until all 8 paillettes are used. After all of the paillettes have been attached, work 1 sc in each rem st.

SECTION 4: Cont to work 1 sc in every st with yarn B (55 sts) until piece measures 3¼" (8cm) from beg.

SECTION 5: Switch to yarn A (stranded with Laisa, if desired) and work 1 sc in every st (55 sts) for 1 row.

SECTION 6: Work 1 sc in the next 8 sts, switch to the smaller hook and attach a bead (see Crochet 101, pages 22–23). Cont to work 1 sc in every st and add a bead every 7 sts until 8 beads are used. Finish the row by working 1 sc in each rem st with the larger hook.

SECTION 7: Starting in second ch from hook, cont to work 1 sc in every st (55 sts) with yarn A for 2 more rows.

SECTION 8: Switch to yarn B and cont to work 1 sc in every st until piece measures 16" (41cm) from beg. On the following row, work 1 sc in each of the next 20 sts, switch to the smaller crochet hook and attach a bead. Work 1 sc in the next 5 sts and attach another bead. Work 1 sc in the next 5 sts and attach the final bead for that row. Cont to work 1 sc in each rem st. Work 1 sc in every st (55 sts) for 2 rows. At the beginning of the next row, work 1 sc in the next 15 sts, and then attach a bead. Attach 2 more beads, working 1 sc in each of the 5 sts between beads. Cont to work 1 sc in each st (55 sts) until pieces measures 22" (56cm) from beg. Cut yarn and tie off.

Finishing

PLACE MARKERS FOR ARMHOLES
Measure 7" (18cm) from the top of the back down each side and place a safety pin or marker for the armhole openings. Repeat for the front panel.

PLACE MARKERS FOR SHOULDER SEAMS
Measure 6" (15cm) from the top right edge of the front toward the center and place a marker. Repeat for the left side. Repeat for the back.

SEAM SHOULDERS
Pin the front and back panels together with right sides facing. Seam the tops of the front and back together between each marker and the edge of the pieces with a single crochet seam (see diagram, page 92). When making seams, match the yarn used for seaming with the yarn used in the project.

SEAM SIDES
Pin right sides together from armhole marker to bottom. Seam both sides from the marker down to the bottom of the shell with a single crochet seam. Turn shell to the right side.

CROCHET AROUND ARMHOLES
Work 2 rows of sc around each armhole opening (approx 48 sts around each armhole).

ADD EMBELLISHMENT
OPTIONAL: Using Laisa or another similar yarn, single crochet in a zig-zag pattern across the bottom front of the shell. You will insert your hook into the stitch, but make your single crochet stitch on top of the crocheted fabric.

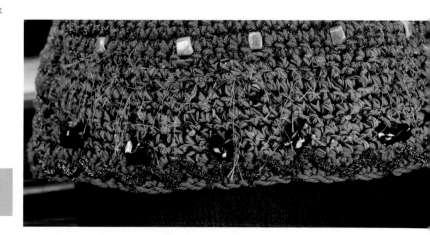

Sparkling Grape Juice Shell

■ ■ ■ I WOULD BE HARD-PRESSED TO PICK A FAVORITE COLOR, but purple definitely makes it into the top three. This variation of the classic shell is worked in vertical stripes of color, which flatter every body type. The sparkle and fizz of the fibers reminds me of sparkling grape juice—you can dress the shell up with tailored slacks or wear it to jazz up a plain pair of jeans. While I like the texture, shimmer and shine of this wardrobe staple, those with more conservative taste can adapt this shell by using a plain ribbon or other fiber of the same gauge.

Yarn

5 skeins (100 yards each) K1C2 Tartelette in Boysenberry (A)

2 balls (120 yards each) K1C2 Crème Brûlée in coordinating color, or any sport weight yarn (B)

1 ball (200 yards) Plymouth Colorlash in variegated purple tones (C)

2 balls (72 yards each) Trendsetter Flora in deep purple (D)

1 ball (149 yards) Trendsetter Aura in deep purple (E)

Hook

6.5mm (K US 10½) crochet hook

Instructions

This shell is worked vertically instead of horizontally like the Deep Blue Sea Shell on page 90. Work 1" to 3" (3cm to 8cm) with each yarn or yarns, as indicated. The finished measurements for this piece are 21" (53cm) long by 19" (48cm) wide.

FRONT AND BACK PANEL (MAKE 2)

FOUNDATION CHAIN: Ch 56 with yarn A.

SECTION 1: Starting in second ch from hook, work 1 sc across all sts (55 sts). Ch 1 and turn work. Cont to work 1 sc in every st (55 sts) for 1" (3cm). Piece measures 1" (3cm) from beg.

SECTION 2: Cut yarn A and join yarn E. Work 1 sc in every st (55 sts) for 1" (3cm). Piece measures 2" (5cm) from beg.

SECTION 3: Cut yarn E and join in yarns B and D. Holding B and D together, work 1 sc in every st (55 sts). Ch 1 and turn work. Cont to work 1 sc in every st (55 sts) for 1" (3cm). Piece measures 3" (8cm) from beg.

SECTION 4: Cut yarns B and D and join in yarn A. With yarn A, work 1 sc in every st (55 sts). Ch 1 and turn work. Cont to work 1 sc in every st (55 sts) for 1" (3cm). Piece measures 4" (10cm) from beg.

SECTION 5: Cut yarn A and join in yarns B and C. Holding B and C together, work 1 sc in every st (55 sts). Ch 1 and turn work. Cont to work 1 sc in every st (55 sts) for 1" (3cm). Piece measures 5" (13cm) from beg.

SECTION 6: Cut yarns B and C and join in yarn A. With yarn A, work 1 sc in every st (55 sts). Ch 1 and turn work. Cont to work 1 sc in every st (55 sts) for 1" (3cm). Piece measures 6" (15cm) from beg.

SECTION 7: Cut yarn A and join in yarns B and D. Holding B and D together, work 1 sc in every st (55 sts). Ch 1 and turn work. Cont to work 1 sc in every st (55 sts) for 1" (3cm). Piece measures 7" (15cm) from beg.

SECTION 8: Cut yarn D and join in yarn C. Holding B and C together, work 1 sc in every st (55 sts). Ch 1 and turn work. Cont to work 1 sc in every st (55 sts) for 1" (3cm). Piece measures 8" (20cm) from beg.

SECTION 9: Cut yarns B and C and join in yarn A. With yarn A, work 1 sc in every st (55 sts). Ch 1 and turn work. Cont to work 1 sc in every st (55 sts) for 2" (5cm). Piece measures 10" (25cm) from beg.

SECTION 10: Cut yarn A and join in yarns B and D. Holding B and D together, work 1 sc in every st (55 sts). Ch 1 and turn work. Cont to work 1 sc in every st (55 sts) for 3" (8cm). Piece measures 13" (33cm) from beg.

SECTION 11: Cut yarns B and D and join in yarn E. With yarn E, work 1 sc in every st (55 sts). Ch 1 and turn work. Cont to work 1 sc in every st (55 sts) for 2" (5cm). Piece measures 15" (41cm) from beg.

SECTION 12: Cut yarn E and join in yarn A. With yarn A, work 1 sc in every st (55 sts). Ch 1 and turn work. Cont to work 1 sc in every st (55 sts) for 1" (3cm). Piece measures 16" (41cm) from beg.

SECTION 13: Cut yarn A and join in yarns B and C. Holding B and C together, work 1 sc in every st (55 sts). Ch 1 and turn work. Cont to work 1 sc in every st (55 sts) for 2" (5cm). Piece measures 18" (46cm) from beg.

SECTION 14: Cut yarn C and join in yarn D. Holding B and D together, work 1 sc in every st (55 sts). Ch 1 and turn work. Cont to work 1 sc in every st (55 sts) for 1" (3cm). Piece measures 19" (48cm) from beg.

SECTION 15: Cut yarns B and D and join in yarn A. With yarn A, work 1 sc in every st (55 sts). Ch 1 and turn work. Cont to work 1 sc in every st (55 sts) for 2" (5cm). Piece measures 21" (53cm) from beg.

Cut yarn and tie off. Weave in all tails.

Finishing

TURN FABRIC VERTICALLY

When you have finished the front and the back side of the shell, lay the pieces out on your work surface so that the stripes run vertically instead of horizontally (see Diagram 2).

PLACE MARKERS FOR ARMHOLES

Measure 7" (18cm) from the top of the back down each side and place a safety pin or marker for the armhole openings. Repeat for the front panel.

PLACE MARKERS FOR SHOULDER SEAMS

Measure 6" (15cm) from the top right edge of the front toward the center and place a marker. Repeat for the left side. Repeat for the back.

SEAM SHOULDERS

Pin the front and back panels together with right sides facing. Seam the tops of the front and back together between each marker and the edge of the pieces with a single crochet seam (see Diagram 2). When making seams, match the yarn used for seaming with the yarn used in the project.

SEAM SIDES

Pin right sides together from armhole marker to bottom. Seam both sides from the marker down to the bottom of the shell with a single crochet seam. Turn shell to the right side.

FINISH EDGES

Work 2 rows of sc around the bottom of the shell, around the neckline and around each armhole opening.

DIAGRAM 1

21" (53CM)

19" (48CM)

SECTION 1	1" (3cm) with A
SECTION 2	1" (3cm) with E
SECTION 3	1" (3cm) with B and D held together
SECTION 4	1" (3cm) with A
SECTION 5	1" (3cm) with B and C held together
SECTION 6	1" (3cm) with A
SECTION 7	1" (3cm) with B and D held together
SECTION 8	1" (3cm) with B and C
SECTION 9	2" (5cm) with A
SECTION 10	3" (8cm) with B and D
SECTION 11	2" (5cm) with E
SECTION 12	1" (3cm) with A
SECTION 13	2" (5cm) with B and C
SECTION 14	1" (3cm) with B and D
SECTION 15	2" (xxcm) with A

DIAGRAM 2

6" (15CM) SHOULDER SEAM

7" (18CM) ARMHOLE

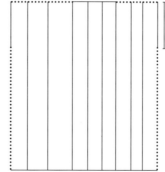

Seam pieces together as indicated by all dotted lines.

Mildred's Stained Glass Window
short-sleeved cardigan

■ ■ ■ MY AUNT MILDRED IS JUST ONE OF THE DYNAMIC, MULTI-TALENTED WOMEN IN MY FAMILY. Her talents include teaching, nursing and cosmetology, to name only a few. And Aunt Mildred loves stained glass windows. Over the years, I have developed a deep appreciation for stained glass myself. If you look closely at stained glass, you'll discover many facets of color and depth of design. When light hits stained glass, the colors look like beautiful precious jewels. Mildred's Stained Glass Window reminds me of the many facets of the precious jewel I have in my own Aunt Mildred.

Yarn

4 hanks (85 yards each) Great Adirondack gossamer ribbon in Kenya

Hooks and Notions

12mm crochet hook

10mm (P US 15) crochet hook

3 dichroic glass buttons

Instructions

This cardigan is worked vertically, from side to side. One size fits most, and the finished measurements are approximately 22" (56cm) wide by 22" (56cm) long. To make the cardigan longer, add to your starting chain. To make the cardigan wider, work more rows. Add eyelash yarn as desired for more texture.

[BACK]

FOUNDATION CHAIN: Using a 12mm hook, ch 39.

REMAINDER: Starting in second ch from hook, work 1 sc in every ch (38 sts). Ch 1 and turn work. Cont to work 1 sc in each st (38 sts) until piece measures 22" (56cm) from beg. Cut yarn and pull tail through.

[FRONT PANEL (MAKE 2)]

FOUNDATION CHAIN: Ch 39.

REMAINDER: Starting in second ch from hook, work 1 sc in every ch (38 sts). Ch 1 and turn work. Cont to work 1 sc in every st (38 sts) until piece measures 12" (30cm) from beg. Cut yarn and pull tail through.

Finishing

PLACE MARKERS

Measure 8" (20cm) from the top of the back down each side and place safety pins or markers on each side. Also measure 8" (20cm) down and place a marker on the outside edge of each front panel.

SHOULDER SEAMS

Align the front panels to the back panel by placing right sides together. Join the front panels to the back panel with a single crochet seam (see Crochet 101, page 29), or use any other seaming method of your choice (see Diagram 3, page 101).

SIDE SEAMS

Pin the front panel pieces to the back piece along the sides. Starting at the markers, join both sides together with a single crochet seam, or use any other seaming method of your choice (see Diagram 3, page 101).

EDGING AND BUTTONS

Turn the cardigan to the right side. Using a 10mm hook, work 2 rows of single crochet around each armhole opening. Work 2 rows of single crochet around the bottom edge of the cardigan. Also work two rows of single crochet around the front edges. Make sure you have the same number of stitches on each side of the front edgings.

Attach buttons where desired on the left front panel of the cardigan. Use natural openings in the crocheted fabric on the opposite front panel as button holes.

DIAGRAM 1 (BACK)

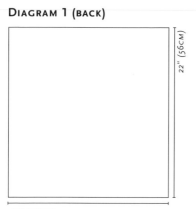

22" (56CM)

22" (56CM)

DIAGRAM 2 (FRONT PANELS)

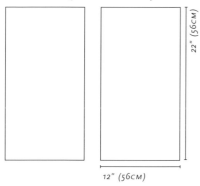

22" (56CM)

12" (56CM)

DIAGRAM 3

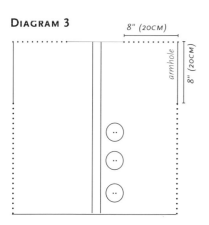

8" (20CM)

armhole

8" (20CM)

Seam pieces together as indicated by dotted lines.

■■■ MY DEAR FRIEND REGINA SUCCUMBED TO BREAST CANCER SEVERAL YEARS AGO. There's a saying that a true friend is more precious than gold, and Regina was truly precious to me. She is no longer physically in my presence, but I have a host of golden memories that are constant reminders of our friendship. Fun, regal and (she'd laugh at this) short, Regina's Gold is one way to treasure my memories of a dear friend. While pink has been associated with the search for a cure for breast cancer, for me, this gold jacket invokes golden memories of friendship, family relationships, sisterhood, and other special bonds, past and present.

Yarn

5 balls (100 yards each) Trendsetter Dolce Ribbon in Yellow Multi (color 110)

7 balls (72 yards each) Trendsetter Joy in Yellow Sunshine (color 1341)

Hook and Notions

20mm crochet hook

4 buttons

Instructions

This is an oversized, one-size-fits-most cropped cardigan. The finished measurements are approximately 33" (84cm) wide by 17" (43cm) long (from top to bottom). It is worked lengthwise (from one side to the other), then turned on its side before seaming. Work one strand of ribbon held together with one strand of Joy throughout. Use the ribbon for all seams.

BACK

FOUNDATION CHAIN: Holding the 2 yarns together, ch 29.

REMAINDER: Holding the 2 yarns together, start in second ch from hook and work 1 sc in every ch (28 sts). Ch 1 and turn work. Cont to work 1 sc in every st (28 sts) until piece measures 33" (84cm) from beg. Cut yarn and pull tail through loop to finish. Weave in all ends.

FRONT PANEL (MAKE 2)

FOUNDATION CHAIN: Holding the 2 yarns together, ch 29.

REMAINDER: Holding the 2 yarns together, start in second ch from hook and work 1 sc in each ch (28 sts). Ch 1 and turn work. Cont to work 1 sc in every st until piece measures 17" (43cm) from beg. Cut yarn and pull tail through loop to finish. Weave in all ends.

Finishing

PIN PIECES TOGETHER

Turn the back piece so the 33" (84cm) side forms the top and bottom (see Diagram 1, page 105). Measure 8" (20cm) down from the top of the back, down the side, and place a marker for the sleeve opening. Do the same on the other side. Also measure 8" (20cm) from the top of each front panel and place a safety pin or marker on each outside edge. Pin the pieces together with right sides facing.

SEAM SHOULDERS

Join the front panels to the back at the shoulder with a single crochet seam (see Crochet 101, page 29), or use any method of your choice (see Diagram 3, page 105).

SIDE SEAMS

Pin the right sides together between the markers. Join the sides together with a single crochet seam, or use any method of your choice (see Diagram 3, page 105).

Attach buttons where desired on the left front panel of the cardigan. Use natural openings in the crocheted fabric opposite the buttons as button holes.

DIAGRAM 1 (BACK)

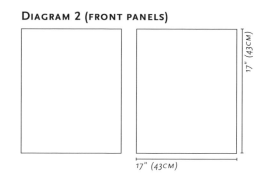

17" (43CM)

33" (84CM)

DIAGRAM 2 (FRONT PANELS)

17" (43CM)

17" (43CM)

DIAGRAM 3

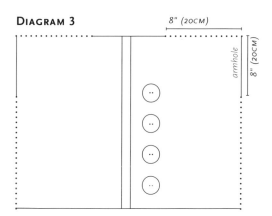

8" (20CM)

armhole

8" (20CM)

Seam pieces together as indicated by dotted lines.

Ice Cream with Rainbow Sprinkles Vest

Use a mocha-colored bulky cotton blend yarn (Crystal Palace Squiggle Print ribbon yarn in Firecracker [color 9296]) and a 10mm hook to create this yummy confection. The mocha-colored ribbon combined with the brightly colored stranders make this short-sleeved cardigan almost good enough to eat. Figure out the gauge for the yarn you choose and adjust the number of stitches in the pattern given accordingly (see Useful Information, page 122). Follow the same instructions as for Regina's Gold to finish the piece.

Lizzy's Night Out Jacket

■ ■ ■ My good friend liz is a one-of-a-kind personality. She is a prolific playwright whose command of the written word elicits a range of thought and emotion that most writers only dream of achieving. She is living every minute of her sixties "on the fringes" and with flair. Lizzy's Night Out is an attempt to capture the unique personality and special energy of Liz. This jacket is youthful, fun, eccentric and elegant. The fringed hem adds excitement. Make this piece, and you are all set for your own night out.

Yarn

15 balls (50 yards each) Gedifra Fashion Trend in gold and black colorway (A)

2 hanks (150 yards each) Blue Sky cotton in black (B)

5 balls (70 yards each) Schachenmayr Nomotta Laisa in black (C)

Hooks and Notions

10mm (P US 15) crochet hook

9mm (M, N US 13) crochet hook

3 large buttons

Instructions

This jacket is made in strips that are later joined together with a single crochet seam. Yarns B and C are stranded together when used. Each strip measures 18" x 5" (46cm x 13cm).

Back and front panels

[strip 1 (make 4)]

Foundation Chain: With yarn A and the 10mm crochet hook, ch 13.

Block 1: Starting in second ch from hook, work 1 sc in each rem ch (12 sts). Cont to work 1 sc in every st until strip measures 6" (15cm) from beg.

Block 2: Cut yarn A and join in yarns B and C. Holding B and C together, work 1 sc in every st (12 sts) until strip measures 12" (30cm) from beg.

Block 3 Switch back to yarn A and cont to work 1 sc in every st until strip measures 18" (46cm) from beg. Cut yarn and tie off.

[strip 2 (make 4)]

Foundation Chain: Holding yarns B and C together, ch 13.

Block 1: Starting in second ch from hook, work 1 sc in every rem ch (12 sts). Cont to work 1 sc in each st until strip measures 6" (15cm) from beg.

Block 2: Switch to yarn A and work 1 sc in all 12 sts until strip measures 12" (30cm) from beg.

Block 3: Cut yarn A and join in yarns B and C. Holding B and C together, cont to work 1 sc in every st until strip measures 18" (46cm) from beg. Cut yarn and tie off.

Sleeves (make 2)

Foundation Row: Holding yarns B and C together, use the 9mm hook to ch 41.

Cuff Rows: Starting in second ch from hook, work 1 sc in every rem ch (40 sts). Ch 1 and turn work. Cont to work 1 sc in every st for 2 rows.

Next and all rem rows: Switch to the 10mm hook and cont to work 1 sc in every st (40 sts) until piece measures 15"(38cm) from beg. Cut yarn and tie off.

Finishing

Use the 9mm hook to join all pieces with a single crochet seam.

SEAM STRIPS TOGETHER

The back is made of 4 strips (see Diagram 1). Place right sides together and seam alternate strips (strip 1, strip 2, strip 1, strip 2). The strips form a checkerboard effect. Each front panel is made up of 2 strips (strip 1, strip 2) (see Diagram 2).

PLACE MARKERS FOR ARMHOLES

Measure 7" (18cm) from the top of the back down each side and place a safety pin or marker for the armhole openings. Repeat for the front panels.

SEAM SHOULDERS

Pin the front panels to the back panel with right sides facing, matching up the edges of the front panels with the edges of the back panel. Seam the tops of the front and back together (see Crochet 101, page 29) to create the shoulder seams (see Diagram 3, page 110).

ATTACH SLEEVES

Place a marker at the top center of each sleeve. (An easy way to find the top center is to simply fold the sleeve in half lengthwise.) With right sides facing, pin the center of each sleeve to the center of each shoulder seam (see Diagram 4, page 110). Seam the sleeves to the body of the jacket with a single crochet seam.

SEAM SIDES AND SLEEVES

Pin the sides together with right sides facing and seam them together with yarn A. Work from start of sleeve to the underarm, then down the side (see Diagram 5, page 110).

ADD BUTTONS

Add buttons to the left side of cardigan (see Diagram 5, page 110), sewing them on with needle and thread.

ADD FRINGE

Cut 24" (60cm) pieces of all of the yarns used in any combination for the fringe. Attach the fringe along the entire bottom of the jacket with a crochet hook as shown in Diagram 5, page 110 (see Crochet 101, pages 24–26). The fringe will be 12" (30cm) long once attached. Trim the ends.

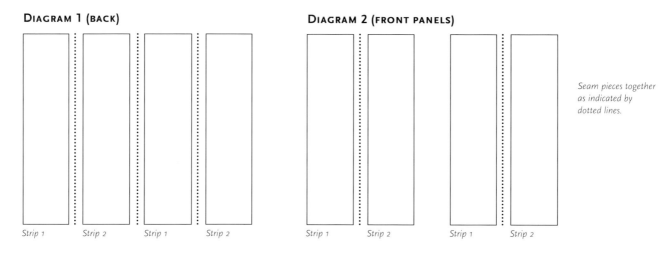

DIAGRAM 1 (BACK)

Strip 1 *Strip 2* *Strip 1* *Strip 2*

DIAGRAM 2 (FRONT PANELS)

Strip 1 *Strip 2* *Strip 1* *Strip 2*

Seam pieces together as indicated by dotted lines.

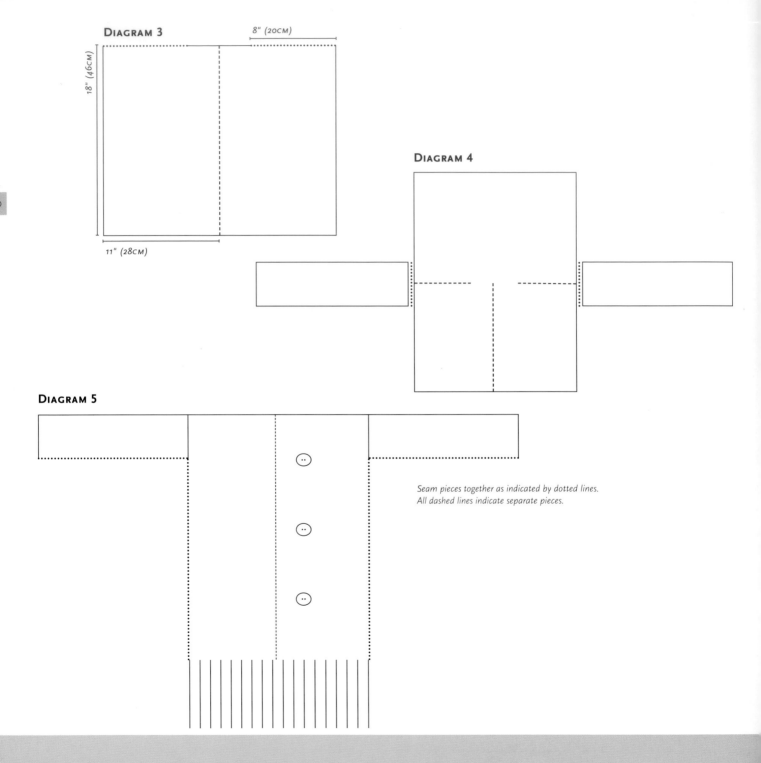

Diagram 3

8" (20cm)

18" (46cm)

11" (28cm)

Diagram 4

Diagram 5

Seam pieces together as indicated by dotted lines.
All dashed lines indicate separate pieces.

Nutmeg and Cinnamon Jacket

Eyelash yarn stranded with a variegated yarn throughout adds flair and style to this oversized jacket. I used Schachenmayr LaNova in Reds (color 87) and Crystal Palace Fizz in Flame (color 7128). Use a 9mm hook to crochet all pieces. Make two front panels measuring 12½" (32cm) wide by 42" (107cm) long. Crochet a back panel 25" (64cm) wide and 42" (107cm) long. Sleeves should be 11" (28cm) wide by 16" (41cm) long. To calculate the number to chain for each piece, make a 4" x 4" (10cm x 10cm) gauge swatch. Count how many stitches make one row and one column and divide each number by four. This number is the gauge, or the number of stitches per inch. Multiply the gauge by the width of each piece and work in single crochet to the desired length. Refer to the Strawberries in Paris jacket on page 112 for detailed instructions on piecing a jacket together.

Strawberries and Cream in Paris
long-sleeved jacket

■ ■ ■ WE ALL DESERVE A SPECIAL TREAT NOW AND THEN, AND THIS JACKET IS JUST THAT.
Laines Anny Blatt, the manufacturer of the featured yarns in this scrumptious creation, originally based in France, has provided high-end, high-quality yarns since the 1920s. The fibers used to create this wearable art masterpiece give an haute couture look to the finished design. When I saw these colors, I immediately thought of strawberries. The fluffy angora adds a creamy feel to this multi-textured fiber blend. And thinking of fashion runways and haute couture naturally led me to Strawberries and Cream in Paris. So, until you are sipping cappuccino at a café in France, enjoy Strawberries and Cream in Paris at home.

Yarn

Approximately 2,600 yards of assorted fibers, worsted to chunky, in various textures. The jacket shown is made with:

3 balls (116 yards each) Laines Anny Blatt Angora in Flamant Ros (A)

1 ball (90 yards each) Gedifra California Colors in Coral (B)

2 spools (109 yards each) Laines Anny Blatt Victoria in Ruben (C)

2 balls (90 yards each) Gedifra Fiocco in Reds (D)

3 balls (125 yards each) Lang Musica in Brick Red (E)

2 hanks (132 yards each) Cascade Pastaza in Poppy (F)

1 hank (220 yards each) Cascade 220 in Coral (G)

1 ball (219 yards each) Laines Anny Blatt Muguet in Grenade (H)

2 hanks (220 yards each) Cascade 220 in Orange (I)

1 ball (88 yards each) Online Punta in Coral 34 (J)

2 balls (61 yards each) Laines Anny Blatt Fleur in Beryl (K)

Optional: 1 ball each

Trendsetter Joy in red

Burgundy Eyelash

Coral Eyelash

Hooks and Notions

9mm (M, N US 13) crochet hook

10mm (P US 15) crochet hook

3 to 5 buttons

Instructions

This is a multifiber jacket that is worked vertically. If you are "color-coordination challenged" or aren't quite ready to experiment, refer to the yarn list or get assistance from the folks at your local yarn shop.

This is an oversized, one-size-fits-most garment. Smaller body types can omit stripes and larger body types can add stripes for a more personalized fit. The large stripes in this design are punctuated by narrow stripes worked with a textured and smooth yarn held together. To create these narrow strips, after Sections 2, 3 and 4, work one row holding yarns K and F together. You will create three vertical, textured stripes down the center of the back of the jacket.

Before you begin crocheting, make sure to read through this entire pattern. This really is a simple pattern, but if you want to simplify it further, you can use fewer stripes or fewer fibers. Another way to simplify the process is to create your own balls of yarn by winding the yarns specified to be used together into separate balls before you begin to crochet. Your customized balls of yarn will be made up of 2 to 3 strands of yarn. When the pattern calls for you to switch yarns, you'll simply pick up one new ball of yarn instead of juggling 2 or 3 separate balls.

Marsha's Corner

If you would like to try creating your own design arrangement, try these tips: First decide how many different fibers you would like to use. Next decide how many stripes you would like. They can be broader or narrower than the ones pictured. Finally, lay your yarns next to each other in the order you would like the stripes to occur. You may also glue or tape your fibers to the chart for a better idea of how various fibers will look in the final garment.

BACK

FOUNDATION CHAIN: Using the 10mm hook and holding 2 strands of A and 1 strand of B together, ch 51.

SECTION 1: Holding 2 strands of A and 1 strand of B together, start in second ch from hook and work 1 sc in each rem ch (50 sts). Ch 1 and turn. Cont to work 1 sc in every st until piece measures 4" (10cm) from beg.

SECTION 2: Cut yarns A and B and join in C and D. Holding C and D together, work 1 sc in each rem st (50 sts) until piece measures 8" (20cm) from beg. Ch 1 and turn.

SECTION 3: Cut C and D and switch to yarns K and F. Holding K and F together, work 1 sc across 50 sts for 1 row. Cut yarn K and join in yarn E. Holding E and F together, work 1 sc across 50 sts until piece measures 11" (28cm) from beg. You may also join in a strand of burgundy eyelash yarn, if desired.

SECTION 4: Cut yarn E and join in yarn K. Holding K and F together, work 1 sc across 50 sts. Ch 1 and turn. Cut yarn and switch to G and H and work 1 sc in every st (50 sts) until piece measures 15" (38cm) from beg.

SECTION 5: Cut yarn H and join in yarn B. Holding G and B together, cont to work 1 sc across all sts (50 sts) until piece measures 18" (46cm) from beg. You may also join in a strand of coral eyelash yarn, if desired.

SECTION 6: Cut G and B and switch to 2 strands of A and 1 strand of B. Holding A and B together, work 1 sc in every st until piece measures 22" (56cm) from beg. Cut yarn and tie off.

YARN KEY:

A: Flamont Ros Angora

B: California Colors in Coral

C: Victoria in Rubens

D: Fiocco in Reds

E: Lang Musica in Brick Red

F: Cascade Pastaza in Poppy

G: Cascade 220 in Coral

H: Muguet in Grenade

I: Cascade 220 in Orange

J: Online Punta in Coral

K: Fleur in Beryl

DIAGRAM 1 (BACK)

SECTION 1	SECTION 2	1 row K and F held together	SECTION 3	1 row K and F held together	SECTION 4	1 row K and F held together	SECTION 5	SECTION 6
4" (10cm) 2 strands of A and 1 strand of B held together	4" (10cm) C and D held together		3" (8cm) E and F held together		4" (10cm) G and H held together		3" (8cm) G and B held together	4" (10cm) 2 strands of A and 1 strand of B held together

FRONT PANELS

Each front panel is slightly different, but you could also choose to make them symmetrical. After each section in the front panels, work one row holding yarns K and F together to create vertical, textured stripes between each color block.

[FRONT PANEL 1]

FOUNDATION CHAIN: Using the 10mm hook and holding 2 strands of A together with 1 strand of Joy, if desired, ch 51.

SECTION 1: Holding 2 strands of A together (plus Joy, if desired), start in second ch from hook and work 1 sc across rem 50 ch. Cont in sc until piece measures 2" (5cm) from beg.

SECTION 2: Cut yarn and join in yarns I, E and H. Holding I, E and H together, work 1 sc across rem 50 sts until piece measures 4" (10cm) from beg.

SECTION 3: Cut yarns I and H and join in yarn J. Holding yarns J and E together, work 1 sc in every st (50 sts) until piece measures 6½" (17cm) from beg.

SECTION 4: Cut yarn and join in F stranded with burgundy eyelash, if desired. Holding F and eyelash (if desired) together, work 1 sc in every st (50 sts) until piece measures 9½" (24cm) from beg.

SECTION 5: Cut yarn F and join in yarns I, E and H. Holding I, E and H together, cont in sc until piece measures 11½" (29cm) from beg.

SECTION 6: Switch to yarns F and C and work 1 sc in every st (50 sts) for 1 row. Cut yarn, tie off and weave in all tails.

[FRONT PANEL 2]

After each section, work one row holding yarns K and F together to create vertical, textured stripes between each color block.

FOUNDATION CHAIN: Using the 10mm hook and holding 2 strands of A together with 1 strand of Joy, if desired, ch 51.

SECTION 1: Starting in the second ch from hook, work 1 sc in rem 50 ch. Cont to work 1 sc in every st (50 sts) until piece measures 2½" (6cm) from beg.

SECTION 2: Cut yarns and join in 2 strands of I and 1 strand of H. Holding I and H together, cont in sc until piece measures 3½" (9cm) from beg.

SECTION 3: Cut yarns I and H and join in yarns E and F. Holding E and F together, cont in sc until piece measures 5½" (14cm) from beg. You may also add in burgundy eyelash, if desired.

SECTION 4: Cut yarn E and join in yarn C. Holding C and F together, work 1 sc across rem 50 sts until piece measures 7½" (19cm) from beg.

DIAGRAM 2 (FRONT PANEL 1)

SECTION 1	SECTION 2	SECTION 3	SECTION 4	SECTION 5	SECTION 6
2" (5cm) 2 strands of A and 1 strand of Joy held together	2" (5cm) I, E and H held together	2½" (6cm) J and E held together	3" (7cm) F and burgundy eyelash held together	2" (5cm) I, E and H held together	1 row F and C held together

DIAGRAM 3 (FRONT PANEL 2)

SECTION 1	SECTION 2	SECTION 3	SECTION 4	SECTION 5	SECTION 6	SECTION 7
2½" (6cm) 2 strands of A and 1 strand of Joy held together	1" (3cm) 2 strands of I and 1 strand of H held together	2" (5cm) F and E held together	2" (5cm) F and C held together	2" (5cm) 2 strands of I and 1 strand of Joy held together	1½" (4cm) 2 strands of I and 1 strand of E held together	1½" (4cm) 2 strands of E and 1 strand of H held together

SECTION 5: Cut C and F and join in 2 strands of I held together with 1 strand of Joy, if desired. Holding I and Joy (if desired) together, work 1 sc in every st (50 sts) until piece measures 9½" (24cm) from beg.

SECTION 6: Cut Joy and join in 1 additional strand of I held together with 1 strand of E. Holding I and E together, work 1 sc across every st (50 sts) until piece measures 11" (28cm) from beg.

SECTION 7: Cut yarn I and join in 1 additional strand of E held together with 1 strand of H. Holding E and H together, work 1 sc in every st (50 sts) until piece measures 12½" (32cm) from beg.

Cut yarn, tie off and weave in all tails.

SLEEVES (MAKE 2)

Start the sleeves with the 9mm hook to give the appearance of shaping.

FOUNDATION CHAIN: Using the 9mm hook and holding 1 strand of K and 1 strand of B together, ch 41.

SECTION 1: Holding K and B together, start in second ch from hook and work 1 sc across rem 40 ch.

SECTION 2: Cut yarn I and join in yarns G and J. Switch to the 10mm hook and hold yarns G and J together. Work 1 sc across all sts (40 sts) until piece measures 3" (8cm) from beg.

SECTION 3: Cut yarn G and join in yarn H. Holding yarns J and H togehter, work 1 sc in every st (40 sts) until piece measures 5" (13cm) from beg.

SECTION 4: Cut yarn H. Join in 1 strand of Joy, if desired. Holding yarn J and Joy together, work 1 sc in every st (40 sts) until piece measures 6" (15cm) from beg.

SECTION 5: Cut yarns J and Joy and join in yarns F and C. Holding F and C together, work 1 sc in each st (40 sts) until piece measures 8" (20cm) from beg.

SECTION 6: Cut yarns F and C and join in 2 strands of E held together with 1 strand of coral eyelash, if desired. Holding E and eyelash (if desired) together, work 1 sc in each st (40 sts) until piece measures 9" (23cm) from beg.

SECTION 7: Cut yarns E and eyelash and join in 2 strands of yarn G and 1 strand of yarn H. Holding G and H together, work 1 sc in each st (40 sts) until piece measures 12" (30cm) from beg.

SECTION 8: Cut yarn G and join in 2 strands of E held together with 1 strand of H. Holding E and H together, work 1 sc in each st (40 sts) until piece measures 14" (36cm) from beg.

SECTION 9: Cut yarn H and join in 1 strand of J. Holding yarns E and J together, work 1 sc in each st (40 sts) until piece measures 16" (41cm) from beg. Cut yarn, tie off and weave in all tails.

DIAGRAM 4 (SLEEVE)

SECTION 1 1 row K and B held together
SECTION 2 3" (8cm) G and J held together
SECTION 3 2" (5cm) G and H held together
SECTION 4 1" (3cm) J and Joy held together
SECTION 5 2" (5cm) F and C held together
SECTION 6 1" (3cm) 2 strands of E and coral eyelash held together
SECTION 7 3" (8cm) 2 strands of G and H held together
SECTION 8 2" (5cm) 2 strands of E and H held together
SECTION 9 2" (5cm) E and J held together

16" (41CM)

14" (36CM)

Finishing

Use the smaller 9mm crochet hook and Cascade 220 in the color of your choice for all seams.

PLACE MARKERS FOR ARMHOLES

Measure 7" (18cm) from the top of the back down each side and place a safety pin or marker for the armhole openings. Repeat for the front panels.

PLACE MARKERS FOR SHOULDER SEAMS

At the top of each front panel, measure 8" (20cm) in from the outside and place marker. Although each front panel is about 10" (25cm) wide, you will leave 2" (5cm) unattached to form a small "flap" that will become a mock lapel when the jacket is finished (see Diagram 5, page 119).

SEAM SHOULDERS

Pin the front panels and back panel together with right sides facing, lining up the sides and tops of all the pieces. Seam the front panels to the back between the markers to create a shoulder seam on each side (see Diagram 5, page 119).

ATTACH SLEEVES

Place a marker at the top center of each sleeve. (An easy way to find the top center is to simply fold the sleeve in half.) With right sides facing, pin the center of each sleeve to the center of each shoulder seam (see Diagram 6, page 119). Join the sleeves to the body of the jacket with a single crochet seam (see Diagram 6, page 119).

SEAM SIDES AND SLEEVES

Pin the sides together with right sides facing and join them with a single crochet seam using Cascade 220 in either color. Work from start of sleeve to the underarm, then down the side (see Diagram 7, page 119).

ADD BUTTONS

If desired, add three or more buttons to the left side of the cardigan, sewing them on with needle and thread (see Diagram 7, page 119).

DIAGRAM 5

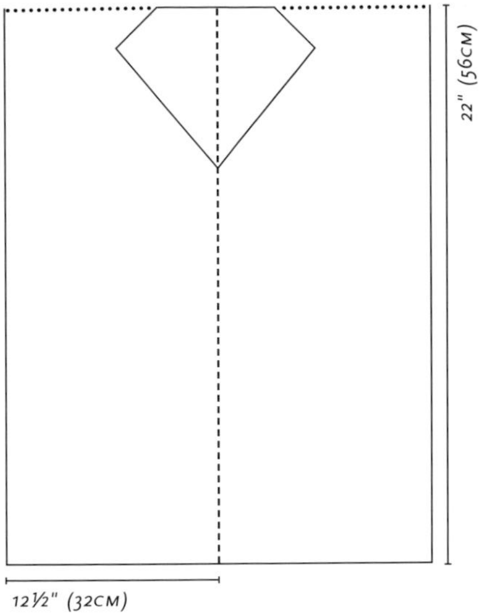

22" (56CM)

12½" (32CM)

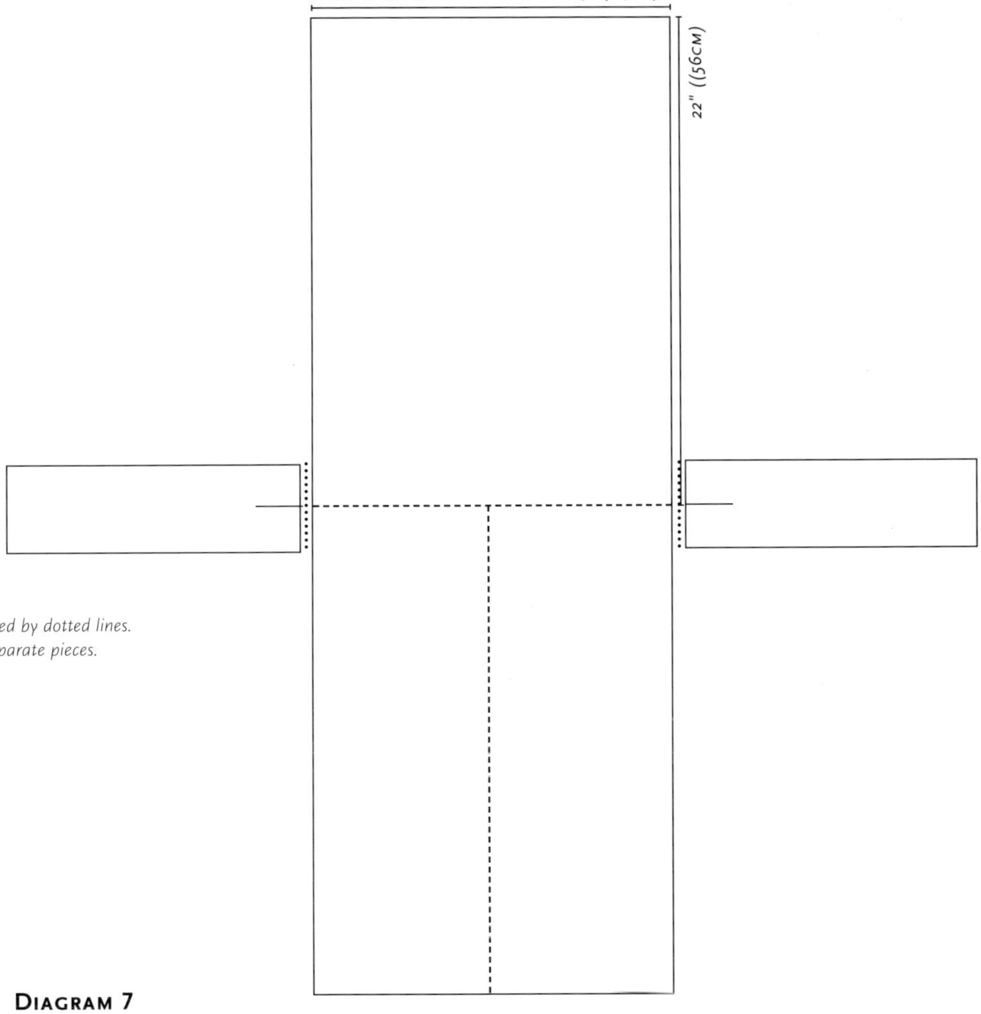

Seam pieces together as indicated by dotted lines.
All dashed lines indicate separate pieces.

DIAGRAM 6

25" (64CM)

22" ((56CM)

DIAGRAM 7

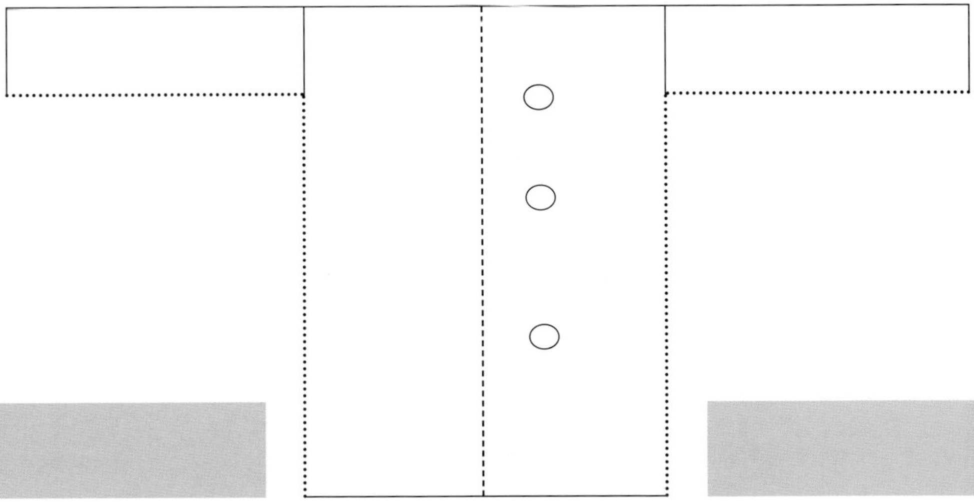

Useful Information

This section is a supplement to the information in the Hook, Line and Sinker section and in the Crochet 101 chapter at the beginning of the book. I hope you use this information as a resource as you crochet the patterns in this book and as you embark on other crochet adventures beyond these pages.

Abbreviations

Although only a few basic abbreviations have been used in the patterns in this book, the following list covers the main abbreviations you might come across in additional crochet patterns as well.

approx	approximately
beg	beginning
ch	chain
cont	continue
dc	double crochet
dec	decrease
dtr	double treble crochet
foll	following
hdc	half double crochet
MC	main color
rem	remaining
rep	repeat
RS	right side
sc	single crochet
sl st	slip stitch
sk	skip
st(s)	stitch(es)
tog	together
trtr	triple treble
WS	wrong side
yo	yarn over
*	repeat instructions after an asterisk or between asterisks as many times as instructed

Crochet Hook Conversions

Finding the correct size of crochet hook can sometimes be confusing. Millimeters, letters, US number sizes...they are as fickle as sunshine in March. I always go by the millimeter size because I find it the most consistent measurement. Below is a chart of the standard measurements and their equivalents.

MILLIMETER SIZE	LETTER SIZE	US NUMBER SIZE
2.25mm	B	1
2.5mm	C	2
3mm	D	3
3.5mm	E	4
4mm	F	5
4.25mm	G	6
4.5mm		7
5mm	H	8
5.5mm	I	9
6mm	J	10
6.5mm, 7mm	K	10½
8mm	L	11
9mm	M, N	13
10mm	P	15
15mm	P, Q	
16mm	Q	
19mm	S	

Substituting Yarns

A Word about Yarn Selection

Although patterns almost always list a specific yarn to use, it is sometimes neccessary to make substitutions. Sometimes types or colors of yarn may be discontinued. Or the listed yarn for any pattern may be cost-prohibitive. Or perhaps you just have your heart set on using yarn from your stash. Whatever the reason, most crocheters will need to make a yarn substitution at some point. The following chart offers you a guideline to follow when substituting yarns for the projects in this book.

FEATURED YARN	COMPARABLE YARN
Hannah Silk Ribbon	$7/16"$ to $1/2"$ (11mm to 13mm) ribbon yarn
Trendsetter Eyelash or Metal Lash yarn	any "thread" type eyelash yarn
Trendsetter Joy	"flag" lash yarn
Trendsetter Dolce/Dolcino Ribbon or Di.ve Orientale	medium-weight ribbon yarn
Anny Blatt Angora	any DK to light worsted angora or certain mohairs
Gedifra Fiocco or Lang Musica	cotton worsted to slightly chunky
Anny Blatt Muguet	any short-haired fiber
Unger Vegas	eyelash yarn with a thicker core strand

Gauge

When you do choose to substitute one yarn for another, you may need to make some adjustments in the pattern if the gauge of the substituted yarn is different from the gauge of the suggested yarn. To keep things simple, the projects in *Crochet Squared* are one size fits most. Even if you don't have access to the yarns suggested for a project, as long as the yarn you choose is fairly similar, the project should turn out just fine. But it is still suggested that you make a gauge swatch before beginning your project. If the yarn you choose is quite a bit different than the yarn listed for the project, it is imperative to crochet a gauge swatch before you begin.

To make a gauge swatch, simply crochet a 4" x 4" (10cm x 10cm) piece of fabric in single crochet. Then count how many stitches and how many rows make up the 4" (10cm) sqaure. Divide each of these numbers by four to come up with the gauge. Simply stated, the gauge is the number of stitches per inch and the number of rows per inch for any given yarn and hook combination. Adjust the pattern accordingly.

Fiber Art: A Poem

by E.J. Foster

A SPECIAL POEM FOR ALL WHO LOSE THEMSELVES IN THE WORLD OF YARN AND FIBER.

Honey, I am now just back from my walk.
Have you per chance taken a look at the clock?
    O my, O my, just look at the time!
    I can't stop now, this sweater's in its prime.
Just stop for a moment—you've been up there all day.
Take some time for yourself, there's got to be a way.
    I can't stop now, I'm almost done.
    Tomorrow I'll stop and look at the sun.
    Did you like the scarf? I made it for you.
    I made it in your favorite color, blue.
Yes, honey, I like it, I wore it today.
But you see, well, what I am trying to say…
    OK, OK, I am on my way.
    I will not dawdle, I am coming, OK?
    Just as soon as I can find a place to stop,
    There are stitches, you know, I mustn't drop.
    Working with fibers is so relaxing to me.
    I tell you what, I'll make us some tea.

Yes, that will be good and very nice.
I think I would like some of that orange spice.
Mom wore that sweater you made her today.
It looked real nice on her, and by the way,
Every eye that sweater caught,
She made sure she told them it wasn't store bought.

She said that you made it in two days real fast.
She said it was specially made, and that it would last.
When they called it a sweater, Mom got real mad.
She acted as if the word sweater was bad.
She said that you made it, that set it apart.
She said, "It isn't a sweater, it's great FIBER ART!"

Resources

Look for the yarns and crochet hooks used to make the projects in this book in your local yarn and craft stores. If you have trouble locating a specific product, contact one of the supply sources listed below to find a local or Internet vendor, or to request a catalog. In addition, the professional staff at Fibergé (The Gathering Place for the Fiber Arts) has put together special yarn kits for the projects featured in *Crochet Squared*.

ANNY BLATT USA, INC.
7796 Boardwalk
Brighton, MI 48116
www.annyblatt.com

ARTEMIS EXQUISITE EMBELLISHMENTS
Distributor of Hanah Silk Ribbons
1.888.233.5187
www.artemisinc.com

BLUE MOON BEADS
7855 Hayvenhurst Ave.
Van Nuys, CA 91406
www.bluemoonbeads.com

BLUE SKY ALPACAS, INC.
P.O. Box 387
St. Francis, MN 55070
www.blueskyalpacas.com

BROWN SHEEP CO., INC.
100662 County Rd. 16
Mitchell, NE 69357
www.brownsheep.com

CASCADE YARNS
1224 Andover Park E.
Tukwila, WA 98188
www.cascadeyarns.com

CLAUDIA HAND PAINTED YARNS
1866 C East Market St. #161
Harrisonburg, VA 22801
www.claudiaco.com

CRYSTAL PALACE YARNS
160 23rd St.
Richmond, CA 94804
www.straw.com

FIBERGÉ: THE GATHERING PLACE FOR THE FIBER ARTS
702 Indian Hill Rd.
Terrace Park, Ohio 45174
513.831.9276
www.fiberge.com
pre-packaged kits

FIRE MOUNTAIN GEMS AND BEADS
1 Fire Mountain Way
Grants Pass, OR 97526-2373
1.800.423.2319
www.firemountaingems.com

IRONSTONE YARNS
P.O. Box 8
Las Vegas, NM 87701

KNITTING FEVER, INC.
35 Debevoise Ave.
Roosevelt, NY 11575
www.knittingfever.com

MANGO MOON
412 N. Coast Hwy #114
Laguna Beach, CA 92651
www.mangomoonyarns,com

PLYMOUTH YARN
P.O. Box 28
Bristol, PA 19007
www.plymouthyarn.com

ROWAN, JAEGER WESTMINSTER FIBERS
4 Townsend W. Unit 8
Nashua, NH 03063
www.knitrowan.com

TAHKI-STACY CHARLES AND FILATURA DI CROSA
70-30 80th St. Building 36
Ridgewood, NY 11384
www.tahkistacycharles.com

TRENDSETTER YARNS
16745 Saticoy St. #101
Van Nuys, CA 91406
www.trendsetteryarns.com

Crocheting on the Web

Go to any Internet search engine and type in "yarn" or "crochet" and you'll literally come up with millions of hits. The Internet is an amazing resource for fiber artists. You'll find lots of places to buy yarn, plus free patterns and helpful Web sites if you get stuck. Of course, it's always best to buy yarn in person from your local yarn store, but who can resist some supplemental online shopping?

YARNXPRESS.COM
WWW.YARNXPRESS.COM

Check out this Web site to buy designer and novelty yarns at a deep discount, often half the retail price. Visit the site often, as selections change almost daily. Many closeout or discontinued brands of yarn are featured here. Yarns are helpfully categorized by three different criteria: fiber content, gauge and manufacturer.

In addition to yarn, the site also sells crochet hooks and knitting needles, kits, accessories, and buttons and hardware. Click on the "patterns" button to find free patterns and patterns for sale.

YARN MARKET
WWW.YARNMARKET.COM

On this Web site, you'll find yarn. And lots of it. Browse Yarn Market's "yarn finder" to search for yarn by brand, gauge, fiber content, texture and even by color family. You can navigate the site by clicking on the categories at the top of the page or by choosing one of the featured items on the home page.

Yarn Market also sells books and patterns, gifts, needles, tools and accessories, and kits. There is a selection of free patterns as well.

YARNZILLA
WWW.YARNZILLA.COM

This site, run by a Minnesota-based yarn store, offers a wide variety of yarns and fibers produced by some of the most popular yarn manufacturers. Knitting and crochet books and patterns are also for sale at the site. And if you're not in the shopping mood, you can amuse yourself by browsing the owners' blog. Look for Yarnzilla's sales and specials.

YARN LADY
WWW.YARNLADY.COM

The Yarn Lady Web site is the online store for the California-based yarn shop of the same name. Check out this site when you need designer yarns, such as Trendsetter. Much of the information on the Web site pertains to the California store, but if you click on the "online store" button at the top of the home page, you'll arrive directly at the yarns for sale.

CROCHET GUILD OF AMERICA
WWW.CROCHET.ORG

The Crochet Guild of America's Web site is a good resource for crocheters of all abilities, from novice to expert. Although there are some patterns and some how-to information for learning and teaching crochet, the site's primary purpose is to post crochet news and events. Browse this Web site to keep up with what is happening in the world of crochet, from the annual national conferences to crochet exhibits and guild meetings across the country.

Index

A

Abbreviations, 121
Accessories
  Bouncing Baby Boy
  Cap + Cardigan, 64
  Green Peas and Grape Juice
  Baby Sweater and Booties, 75
  Jessica-Loves-Chocoloate Purse, 80
  Let's-Go-Shopping Tote, 84
  Miriam's Savvy Black Fuzzy
  Chenille Hat, 71
  Pastel Paradise Slippers, 78
  "That's My Baby" Booties, 72
  Vallarie's Royal Slippers, 76
  Vickie's Bad Hair Day Cap, 68
  Yoruba Handbag, 83

B

Baby clothes
  Bouncing Baby Boy
  Cap + Cardigan, 64
  Green Peas and Grape Juice Baby
  Sweater and Booties, 75
  "That's My Baby" Booties, 72
Berries and Champagne Shawl, 34
Body drapes
  Penny-for-Your-Thoughts Copper
  Beaded Body Drape, 38
  Red Hot Body Drape, 41
Body Wraps, 32
  Berries and Champagne Shawl, 34
  Claudia's Hand Shrawl, 48
  Grass Is Greener Ponshawl, The,
  46
  Kathleen's Peacock Ponshawl, 42
  Kimmy-Kimmy KoKo Pop Silk
  Scarf, 34
  Miter Square Shrawl, 58

Ocean Mist Shrawl, 52
Orange You Glad Shrawl, 53
Painter's Palette Poncho, 54
Penny-for-Your-Thoughts Copper
Beaded Body Drape, 41
Pride and Soy Ponshawl, 47
Red Hot Body Drape, 41
Bouncing Baby Boy Cap + Cardigan,
64

C

Cardigans
  Bouncing Baby Boy Cardigan, 67
  Mildred's Stained Glass Window
Short-Sleeved Cardigan, 98
Changing Colors, 28
Claudia's Hand Shrawl, 48
Crochet 101, 14
  Adding Fringe, 24 See also Fringe
  Changing Colors, 28
  Crocheting with Beads, 22
  Crocheting with Paillettes, 20
  Making a Chain, 15
  Making a Slip Knot, 14
  Miter Square, 31
  See also Miter Square
  Holding Two Yarns Together, 19
  Joining Squares with Single
  Crochet Seam, 29
  Single Crochet Stitch, 16
  Weaving in Ends, 30
  Working with Eyelash Yarn, 19
Crocheting on the Web, 120
Crocheting with Beads, 22
  Deep Blue Sea Beaded Shell, 90
Crocheting with Paillettes, 20
  Berries and Champagne Shawl, 37

D–G

Deep Blue Sea Beaded Shell, 90
Fiber Art: A Poem, 123
Fringe
  Basic Fringe, 24
  Individual Beaded Fringe, 27
  Tassel Fringe, 26
Get Hip to Squares, 7
Grass Is Greener Ponshawl, The, 46
Green Peas and Grape Juice Baby
Sweater and Booties, 75

H

Hat sizing chart, 70
Hats
  Bouncing Baby Boy Cap, 64
  Miriam's Savvy Black Fuzzy
  Chenille Hat, 71
  Vickie's Bad Hair Day Cap, 68
Holding Two Yarns Together, 19
Hook, 8
  conversion chart, 122
  holding, 9
  types of, 8
Hook Conversion Chart, 122
Hook, Line and Sinker, 8

I–K

Ice Cream with Rainbow Sprinkles
Vest, 105
Jessica-Loves-Chocolate Purse, 80
Joining Sqaures with Single
Crochet Seam, 29
Kathleen's Peacock Ponshawl, 42
Kimmy-Kimmy KoKo Pop Silk Scarf,
34

L–N

Let's-Go-Shopping Tote, 84
Line, 10 *See also* Yarn
Lizzy's Night Out Jacket, 106
Making a Chain, 15
Making a Slip Knot, 14
Mildred's Stained Glass Window
Short-Sleeved Cardigan, 98
Miriam's Savvy Black Fuzzy Chenille
Hat, 71
Miter Square
   making, 31
   shrawl, 58
Miter Square Shrawl, 58
Nutmeg and Cinnamon Jacket, 111

O–P

Ocean Mist Shrawl, 52
Orange You Glad Shrawl, 53
Painter's Palette Poncho, 54
Pastel Paradise Slippers, 78
Penny-for-Your-Thoughts Copper
Beaded Body Drape, 38
Ponchos
   Painter's Palette Poncho, 54
Ponshawls
   Grass Is Greener Ponshawl, The, 46
   Kathleen's Peacock Ponshawl, 42
   Pride and Soy Ponshawl, 47
Ponshawls Galore, 46
Pride and Soy Ponshawl, 47

R

Reading a Pattern, 13 *See also* Sinker
Red Hot Body Drape, 41
Regina's Gold Cropped Jacket, 102
Resources, 124

S

Selecting a Project, 13 *See also* Sinker
Shawls
   Berries and Champagne Shawl, 37
Shells, Cardigans + Jackets, 88
   Deep Blue Sea Beaded Shell, 90
   Ice Cream with Rainbow
   Sprinkles Vest, 105
   Lizzy's Night Out Jacket, 106
   Mildred's Stained Glass Window
   Short-Sleeved Cardigan, 98
   Nutmeg and Cinnamon Jacket,
   111
   Regina's Gold Cropped Jacket, 102
   Sparkling Grape Juice Shell, 94
   Strawberries and Cream in Paris
   Long-Sleeved Jacket, 112
Shrawl for Every Occasion, A, 52
Shrawls
   Claudia's Hand Shrawl, 48
   Miter Square Shrawl, 58
   Ocean Mist Shrawl, 52
Single Crochet Stitch, 16
Sinker, 13
   Reading a Pattern, 13
   Selecting a Project, 13
Sparkling Grape Juice Shell, 94
Strawberries and Cream in Paris
Long-Sleeved Jacket, 112
Substituting Yarns, 122

T–V

"That's My Baby" Booties, 72
Useful Information, 120
   Abbreviations, 121
   Crocheting on the Web, 120
   Fiber Art: A Poem, 123
   Hook Conversion Chart, 122
   Substituting Yarns, 122
Vallarie's Royal Slippers, 76
Vickie's Bad Hair Day Cap, 68

W–Z

Weaving in Ends, 30
Working with Eyelash Yarn, 19
Yarn, 10
   choosing, 11
   holding, 12
   types of, 10
Yoruba Handbag, 83

Check out these other great F+W Publications, Inc. books for inspiration and more fabulous project ideas!

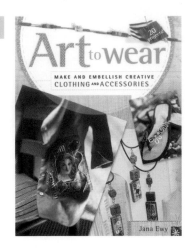

BY JANA EWY

There's no better way to show off your creative talents than to adorn yourself, your family and friends with your own works of art. Whatever your unique style, this book shows you how to create jewelry, accessories and clothing that match your personality. Author Jana Ewy demonstrates how to dress up jackets, sweaters, t-shirts, flip-flops, purses and belts with paint, ink, metal, fabric, fibers, beads and even Chinese coins. You'll be inspired to make your mark on your clothing and accessories by the over 25 projects and variations included in the book.

ISBN-13: 978-1-58180-597-0
ISBN-10: 1-58180-597-7
paperback, 96 pages, 33110

BY CINDY CRANDALL-FRAZIER

Single Crochet for Beginners is a must-have resource book for beginner crocheters or for those who want to teach a friend or family member to crochet. Inside this book, you'll find the basic techniques and stitches you'll need to create over 30 beautiful projects. All of the projects, including hats, mittens and mats, are made with the simple single crochet stitch—easy to master and quick to crochet. You'll also find a quick-facts guide about color and fiber that is useful for selecting yarn for future projects. This comprehensive and portable reference is great to have on hand for all your crochet questions.

ISBN-10: 0-89689-176-3
ISBN-13: 978-0896-891-760
paperback, 128 pages, 00176

BY LISA SHOBHANA MASON

YarnPlay shows you how to fearlessly mix yarns, colors and textures to create bold and graphic knitted items. You'll learn how to draw from your yarn stash to create stylish, colorful knits, including sweaters, tanks, hats, scarves, blankets, washcloths and more for women, men and children. Best of all, you'll learn knitting independence—author Lisa Shobhana Mason believes in learning the rules so you can break them. She teaches you how to take a pattern and make it your own.

ISBN-13: 978-1-58180-841-4
ISBN-10: 1-58180-841-0
paperback with flaps, 128 pages, Z0010